PAIN
AND
PROGRESS

PAIN
AND
PROGRESS

THE FIRST 12 YEARS OF
THE NEW JERSEY DEVILS

Stan & Shirley Fischler

Published by
The New Jersey Devils
Byrne Meadowlands Arena
P.O. Box 504
East Rutherford, New Jersey 07073

Printed in the United States of America

1st printing, 1994

Library of Congress Catalog Number 91-78330

ISBN 1-56352-039-7

This book was printed by Horowitz/Rae, Fairfield, NJ.
The text was set in Clearface by Typo-Repro Service, Inc., Atlanta, Georgia.
Book design by Tonya Beach.
Photo credits: Jim Turner, Steve Crandall, Richard Pilling, Ray Amati, Frank Micelotta, and Bruce Bennett Studios.

Book production by Longstreet Press, Inc., Marietta, Georgia.

To Dr. John J. McMullen and Lou Lamoriello,
without whom none of this would have been possible.

AUTHORS' ACKNOWLEDGMENTS

Like the growth of the Devils, this history required cooperation and diligent behind-the-scenes work.

Without the assistance of key aides, we couldn't have put this manuscript together. With that in mind, we are especially grateful to our research experts Matt Messina and Todd J. Diamond who delivered clutch work in the finest John MacLean manner. Others who were notable in their assistance include: Ashley Scharge, Lou Villano, Adrienne Nardo, Jeff Resnick, Darwin Lee, and Vanessa Kalinoski.

Likewise an immense debt of thanks to Brian Petrovek, Dave Freed, Mike Levine, Nelson Rodriguez, and others in the Devils' public relations department, who have always been generous with their time, cooperation, and patience.

ACKNOWLEDGMENTS II

Because of space requirements, it was impossible to elaborate on all of the individuals who contributed to the PAIN AND PROGRESS, and, no doubt, there will be some folks whose names will accidentally be omitted. For that, we apologize in advance.

We would be remiss in not citing some who were particularly enjoyable with which to deal in their various capacities. These include former President Bob Butera, who was always a gentleman and helpful during his reign.

Play-by-play broadcaster Larry Hirsch gave the club a vocal imprimatur and a grand sense of excitement in those early, difficult years when wins were few and far between. His broadcasting sidekick, Fred Shero — already an institution — was a joy to meet every night in the press room and a pleasure to hear on the air.

From the very beginning, every member of the Devils staff was remarkably cooperative from stickboy on up. Coaches, from Billy McMillan and Doug Carpenter to Jim Schoenfeld, John Cunniff, and Tommy McVie, all made our jobs easier, as did the ever popular Max McNab, one of the most knowledgeable, affable hockey men in captivity.

Broadcasters such as Al Albert, Steve Albert, Mike Emrick, Mike Eruzione, Peter Mahovlich, Sal Messina, Spencer Ross, and Dale Arnold added unforgettable pleasure with their work, as did Chris Moore and Larry Brooks and more recent contemporaries Sherry Ross and Mike Miller. My SportsChannel sidekicks, Gary Thorne and Peter McNab, have made my life a lot more fun and added to my knowledge of the hockey business.

Although they are well mentioned in the book, it would not be redundant to point out that none of this would be possible without the guidance of owner Dr. John J. McMullen and the inspiration of President-General Manager Lou Lamoriello, who conceived this project.

TABLE OF CONTENTS

FOREWORD

If ever the bromide "Pain and progress are inseparable" was applicable for a major league franchise, the New Jersey Devils are Exhibit A.

Few, if any, big-time organizations have undergone so convulsive a start and so many early setbacks as The Garden State's National Hockey League representative.

Conceived in Kansas City and nurtured in Denver, the infant franchise was—if you will excuse the expression—bedevilled by ownership problems from the very beginning.

As the NHL Kansas City Scouts and then the Colorado Rockies, the club lacked the essential element that is required in growth, not only in people but the corporate world itself, and that is stability.

When the Rockies began crumbling in Colorado, it was imperative that the franchise, if it were to be saved, would require a very special savior.

What was needed, essentially, was someone who could lead this outfit out of the hockey wilderness. It required, unlike the situation in previous locations, someone who came from the community and gave a damn about the evolution of this club.

There no longer was room for a fly-by-night entrepreneur. This time there had to be an owner who would display perseverance and grim determination to see the project through to fruition. In plain English, it required a pro; someone who knew the sports business like he knows how to breathe; a personality who thrived on challenges and knew first-hand what a battle was all about.

Then, the National Hockey League and New Jersey hockey fans got lucky.

Dr. John J. McMullen stepped forward, purchasing the Rockies and moving the franchise to The Meadowlands.

What's lucky about that?

For starters, Dr. McMullen made a commitment, and the proof is in the decade of devotion and dogged work he has dedicated to the hockey club.

He also made an investment and not a very small one at that. (If you don't believe it, ask the Rangers, Islanders, and Flyers.)

Dr. McMullen knew what fighting is all about. He's a Navy man. He served in World War II through 1954, when he left the service with the rank of commander.

He knew what business was all about, too. From scratch, he built one of the nation's most impressive and respected naval architecture and marine engineering concerns.

And he knew New Jersey. A native of Montclair, Dr. McMullen has been a lifelong resident of the state and was determined to give its fans a world-class product.

To say it wouldn't be easy would be the understatement of the half-century. By the time the franchise was renamed and installed at Byrne Arena, previous management had stripped it of draft choices and left a roster ravaged to the very bone.

Yet this was the franchise that entered the league when its Trans-Hudson rivals had reached their competitive peak. Al Arbour's Islanders were enroute to their fourth consecutive Stanley Cup, and the Rangers, under Herb Brooks, had one of the NHL's most imposing sextets.

Dr. McMullen never flinched. Employing the slogan of the World War II U.S. Navy Seebees—"CAN DO!"—he got down to the business of revitalizing the franchise.

Oh, it was painful, to be sure. A deceptively competitive opening season was followed by an enormous letdown in Year Two. The 1983-84 campaign was pockmarked with the infamous Wayne Gretzky "Mickey Mouse" remark and an agonizing ten-game losing streak.

Still, there were tangible results. Slowly but inexorably, a nucleus of devoted fans was growing. They understood Dr. McMullen's dilemma and rode with the blows, and, eventually, a flicker was seen at the ends of the Holland and Lincoln Tunnels. It grew as the Devils acquired the likes of John MacLean, Kirk Muller, Bruce Driver, and Ken Daneyko.

Under the management of Max McNab and coaching of Doug Carpenter, tangible progress was evident, but every New Jersey fan knew—as any Rangers fan could confirm—that there were two objectives in this ice game: make the playoffs and win the Stanley Cup.

Carpenter didn't quite have the formula. Dr. McMullen was patient, to be sure. After three seasons of futility, the redhead remained behind the bench, but then the owner engineered THE move that would finally put the franchise in the fast lane.

Lou Lamoriello, a veritable institution running hockey teams and the athletic program at Providence College, was lured to East Rutherford to author a winning script for the Devils. As president and general manager, Lamoriello immediately made an impact trade, instilled his no-nonsense philosophy on the organization, and set it in motion.

When it was evident a catalyst was necessary in January 1988, he installed Jim Schoenfeld as coach. The move catapulted the Devils into the playoff race and led to one of the most extraordinary miracle finishes professional hockey has known.

There remained glitches, to be sure but, under Lamoriello, the Devils had become a team to be taken seriously. In the past seven years they have gained a playoff berth six times, something that was unthinkable in the early years of the franchise.

With Dr. McMullen's guidance, the Devils daringly imported three Soviet players and were at the forefront of what became known as the NHL's Russian Revolution.

In a sense it's hard to believe that ten years have past since Chico Resch, Hector Marini, Steve Tambellini, and Bob Lorimer were wearing the red, green, and white of New Jersey. So much has happened so quickly.

What we have attempted to do in this history is bring to life the events—big and small— that molded the Devils into what they are today—a club that has weathered adversity and now takes dead aim at the most coveted prize of all, the Stanley Cup.

Stan and Shirley Fischler

1

THE ROOTS OF HOCKEY IN NEW JERSEY

Crowds cheer lustily for a goal in the waning minutes of a tightly played game.

An explosion of sound shakes the arena wall as the vulcanized rubber disk eludes the netminder's desperate lunge and skims over the goal line.

Ooohs and ahhhs signal the throbbing heartbeats as bodies crunch against bodies.

Sounds like another major league hockey game at Byrne Arena, doesn't it?

And well it should, because that is the brand of ice ambience to which we have become accustomed in the Decade of the Devils.

In fact, these sights and reverberations emanate from a dim, distant era. Women were wearing skirts to their ankles at the time. Men were adorned with straw hats—fedoras in winter—and spats (those neat, gray leather coverings that extended from the top of the shoe to the ankle). The automobile was in its infancy and hockey—yes, hockey—was booming in New Jersey.

Difficult as it may be to imagine, The Ice Game's roots in the Garden State date back to the 19th century. The refrigeration plant which guaranteed artificial ice in covered rinks already has been popularized by Frank and Lester Patrick, the latter of whom is Craig Patrick's grandfather.

Frank and Lester introduced their wonder rinks to Pittsburgh and other points east, and thus hockey became an "in" sport among select precincts along the Eastern Seaboard.

Hockey's popularity soared after the turn of the century when Canadian touring teams such as the internationally renowned Ottawa Senators visited New York City for a historic exhibition series in Manhattan's St. Nicholas Arena. The visit drew raves, packing the 7,000-seat arena and winning headlines in the local dailies. The New York *Times* toasted Ottawa ace Cylone Taylor as "The Ty Cobb of Hockey," linking him with one of the best baseball players of the day.

Meanwhile, hockey's collegiate version was in the early throes of expansion, and New Jersey sported one of the better university squads. Princeton was one of five original members of the Intercollegiate Hockey League organized during the winter of 1900. Columbia, Dartmouth, Harvard, and Yale were the other clubs.

Princeton won championships in 1907, 1912, 1913, and 1914. This surprised none of the day's journalists since one of the university's foremost players, starting in the fall of 1910, was one Hobart (Hobey) Baker, the first outstanding player developed in the United States.

The Boston *Herald* was less modest in its appraisal, noting in February 1913 that "Baker is without a doubt the greatest amateur hockey player ever developed in this country or Canada. No player has ever been able to weave in or out of a defense and change his pace and direction with the uncanny generalship of Baker. He is the wonder player of hockey. And above all, he is extremely clean in his work on the ice—he believes that rough stuff has no place in the game."

Baker brought more honors to New Jersey hockey than any player in his era. Upon graduation, he continued starring for the St. Nicholas Hockey Club and then became an aviator in World War I, winning a French "Croix de Guerre" for exceptional valor under fire during the early summer of 1918 shortly before the Armistice.

Just a month after the hostilities ceased in November 1918, Baker took a plane up for a spin, against the wishes of fellow pilots. Hobey died in the ensuing crash.

Baker was permanently memorialized at Princeton with construction of the Hobey Baker Rink where the Tigers began practicing in 1922. Although Princeton produced powerful teams in the late 1920s and early 1930s, the next collegiate championship did not come to New Jersey until 1941 when the Tigers took the Quadrangular League title.

Jerseyites had another brand of hockey to savor in the years preceding World War II, and a terribly exciting version as well. Under the aegis of Thomas F. (Tommy) Lockhart, the Eastern Amateur Hockey League flourished as a feeder to the stronger American League as well as the National Hockey League.

Though it was dubbed "amateur," the EAHL skaters were paid as minor pros and reached a high level of competition. The Eastern League installed an excellent club at Convention Hall in Atlantic City, the Sea Gulls, while another called the River Vale Skeeters provided thrills for Northern New Jersey fans, not to mention one from Newark for a brief period.

The Jersey teams frequently played at Madison Square Garden where the Rangers' EAHL squad, the Rovers, provided the opposition. A number of top performers made their way to the big time from the Sea Gulls and Skeeters, including Hall of Fame referee Roy (Red) Storey who skated for River Vale before the outbreak of World War II.

While the Skeeters disbanded once the war began, never to return, Atlantic City re-entered the league in post-war years as a Rangers' farm team along with the Rovers. One of the best trios in EAHL history—Johnny Flynn, Stan McClellan, and Mauno Kauppi—played for the Sea Gulls.

Princeton also resumed hockey after WWII coached by the widely respected Dick Vaughn who wrote *Hockey*, the definitive manual of the sport, during the 1940s. Vaughn remained the Tigers' mentor until l954 when he was replaced by Norman Wood.

In the early years, participants on the collegiate and amateur level tended to be limited to the middle and upper classes but this changed with the boom in rink construction of the 1950s and 1960s throughout the state.

Typical of the new grass-roots leagues was the West New York Ice Hockey Association which was based in a bizarre-shaped arena overlooking the Hudson River. For inexplicable reasons, its designers laid out an ice surface that was not your typical 200 by 85 feet but rather one that measured 128 feet long by 108 feet wide!

It was hell on goalies who often were called upon to stop accurate slapshots from the goal line at the other end of the rink. Nor was it a lark for defensemen trying to head off end runs around either side.

"When you came to West New York to play hockey," said writer-player Ira Gitler, author of *Hockey From A to Z,* "it was best to be a forward."

Minor pro hockey eventually was seen in Cherry Hill and Haddonfield. A poor man's version of the big-league game was seen at the Cherry Hill Arena in 1974 when the New York Golden Blades of the World Hockey Association went belly-up at its original Madison Square Garden home and relocated under the sobriquet of New Jersey Knights. Cherry Hill's rink was notorious for the unevenness of its ice surface which rose to a hill at center and then tapered off at each side. "It was," said Hall of Famer Bobby Hull who then skated for the Winnipeg Jets, "one of the most bizarre rinks I've ever had the displeasure of skating on; and I've been on some lulus."

So, while New Jersey has yet to be home to a Stanley Cup champion, it has a long, rich hockey heritage. The ice roots run deep, and in time they sprouted in a former marsh called The Meadowlands where a goliath rink would grow and be dubbed The Byrne Meadowlands Arena.

As the girders were welded into place, a groundswell of support for New Jersey's first major professional sport could be heard throughout the National Hockey League. In time, the result would be a hearty NHL welcome for the New Jersey Devils.

After dealing Rob Ramage for two first round picks, Bert Marshall (Left) and MacMillan make Rocky Trottier the Devils first draft choice, though the team had not yet been renamed.

three choice, Pat Verbeek, a center who had scored 37 goals with Sudbury of the Ontario Hockey League.

"He could be the biggest surprise of all," said MacMillan. "He's hard-nosed and very mature."

Training camp opened at Ice World rink in Totowa, New Jersey, on September 11, 1982, as MacMillan attempted to complete a deal that would bring one-time Islanders favorite Garry Howatt to New Jersey. Howatt had made it clear he did not want to play in Hartford where he had been traded.

As players streamed into camp from all parts of Canada and the United States, the Devils roster began taking shape. Among the NHLers, there was Joel Quenneville, Bob Lorimer, Joe Cirella, Aaron Broten, and Steve Tambellini, along with former Islanders goaltender Chico Resch.

A veteran of several shellings as a Colorado Rocky, Resch wasted no time telling reporters how the previous management had hurt the franchise. "They made some bad moves in the past," said Resch. "Many of the mistakes were because of pressure from the former ownership. There were a

lot of panic moves made in an attempt to produce an instant winner. Now we're moving in a positive direction. The only way to accomplish anything in this game is by drafting blue-chip players and being patient with them."

Resch did not sound troubled by the defense in front of him. "Potentially," he went on, "we have as much defensively as three-quarters of the teams in the NHL. But offensively we need help. We're simply not going to win many games by scoring only a couple of goals a game."

Bob Lorimer was more explicit. "If people expect us to be competitive with the Islanders and Rangers this year, they're crazy. On a given day, yes, but not over the course of the season."

Actually, it didn't take very long for the Devils to win a hockey game. On September 17, 1982, they beat the Washington Capitals, 3–1. It was their first game—and first win—since they escaped from the hopeless situation in Colorado and came east.

The historic Devils goal was scored by Randy Pierce, who had been limited to only

Don Lever responds to questions after being named the Devils' first captain on August 20, 1982.

five games the previous season because of injuries and rookie free agent Glenn Merkosky. "This," said a tickled MacMillan, "is a nice, positive way to start a new franchise."

New Jersey fans would be treated to the home exhibition debut of the team on Tuesday night, September 21, 1982. Facing them would be the New York Rangers, a team that would soon become a keen rival. Dr. McMullen accelerated rivalry possibilities by twitting the denizens of Madison Square Garden in a pre-game comment that was well covered by the media.

"I believe we're going to be a lot more aggressive than the Rangers," said Dr. McMullen. "They're complacent because they're sold out."

Seizing on the observation, the *Post* headlined the story RANGERS ANGRY OVER McMULLEN'S REMARK.

Perhaps they were, but Dr. McMullen couldn't have cared less. He wanted his team to put on a good showing against the 56-year-old franchise from across the Hudson River and he was amply rewarded, although the Devils did not win.

Merlin Malinowski scored the first goal for the Devils on home ice, stuffing his own rebound past goalie Steve Baker at 10:24 of the first period. He scored again with 3:31 left in the game, but the Rangers got three goals, enough for the 3–2 margin.

The 9,193 fans were well entertained, although MacMillan was disappointed. "We still have a long way to go," he opined.

MacMillan was trying to persuade Tapio Levo, his only offensive defenseman, to leave his native Finland and rejoin the Devils, and he still was trying to pry Garry Howatt from Hartford. On the positive side was the play of young Daneyko. "He played with poise," said MacMillan. "We used him

Lever and Resch pose with McMullen prior to the home opener vs. Pittsburgh on October 5, 1982; Lever would score the team's first goal just 2:21 into the first period.

in every situation and he handled himself well. So did Pat Verbeek."

In the waiver draft just prior to the official season's opener MacMillan plucked defenseman Carol Vadnais, Dave Hutchison, and Murray Brumwell. Their first foe, at Byrne, would be the Pittsburgh Penguins.

The milestone game saw New Jersey open with the first goal, by Don Lever, at 2:21, followed by another directed home from the stick of Hector Marini at 5:23 of the first. The Penguins counterattacked with three straight goals and led 3–2 until the five-minute mark of the third period.

Malinowski was Merlin on the Spot, tying the count with a shot past Michel Dion at 5:03. From that point on the goaltending held fast and the game ended in a 3–3 draw. The 13,663 in attendance seemed pleased as did the often ascerbic press critics.

"It was almost shocking," said Mark Everson of the *Post*. "The Devils were a tough hockey team and not a laughing stock. Most amazing of all, they didn't lose."

Matter of fact, they wouldn't lose very often in the first weeks of the season. After three games they were undefeated (1–0–2) with four points, only two out of first place. They had beaten the Rangers and came back from a 5–1 deficit to tie Toronto. "It's the most refreshing thing that's ever happened to this franchise," bubbled Chico Resch. "Now the maturity of the team has to show. We have to realize why this has happened."

Nobody expected the upstarts to go through the season undefeated. They were finally brought down by the Montreal Canadiens 5–3, at Byrne Arena but MacMillan wasn't complaining. "Hey, it wasn't going to go on forever. We had to get beaten

Hector Marini would become New Jersey's first All-Star.

sooner or later. I would be very pleased if we lost one out of every four games for the rest of the season." Yes, good things continued to happen to MacMillan & Co. Howatt finally was obtained from Hartford and Tapio Levo skated out of retirement in time for a game against the Penguins in Pittsburgh. This was a wild one.

With 38 seconds remaining and the score knotted at 5–5, Hector Marini wristed a 12-foot shot between the pads of Dion to cap a wild, spectacular 6–5 triumph over the Penguins. Levo assisted on four goals and tied a club record in the process. There were 74 games remaining for New Jersey but already Hector Marini was talking playoffs.

Why were the Devils doing so surprisingly well?

• Hector Marini was scoring clutch goals.

• Tapio Levo gave them a solid offensive defenseman.

• Free agent center Glen Merkosky was proving to be a neat playmaker.

• Newly acquired center Rick Meagher was an excellent defensive forward who also could score.

• MacMillan had his players believing.

"They are for real," MacMillan said of his players. "This team is showing that it isn't going to roll over and play dead for anybody, at home or on the road."

In time The Law of Averages — or the rest of the league, take your pick — would catch up to the Devils and the heady launching of the franchise would run into an NHL minefield. A late October two-game road trip in which they lost twice, including a horrible 3–1 defeat to Winnipeg, set the club back on its heels. They managed only twelve shots on goal and didn't score until the last minute of the play.

"We're a little apprehensive," Resch allowed.

And for good reason. They would soon slip so egregiously that the only race left for them was for fifth place in the six-team Patrick Division. An eight-game winless streak in February 1983 removed any aspirations for a playoff berth and by March 3rd they were one loss from playoff elimination.

Despite the losses, a note of optimism was sounded in the dressing room. "We're making some progress," said Aaron Broten. "Last year we didn't know if the team would be in Denver or wherever. Now we know we're going to be in New Jersey next year."

Joel Quenneville asserted that the club was more "in the games" in 1982-83 than in the previous season. "We still lose," he said, "but last year it would be over in ten minutes."

On the night of March 3rd, the Devils playoff quest was over by the end of the second period. A New Jersey goal by rookie Larry Floyd tied the score 1–1 in the second period before Philadelphia pulled away in the third enroute to a 4–1 win.

The end of the playoff run did not mean the end of the season by any means. MacMillan still had to lay the groundwork for 1983-84 and there was the trade deadline coming up on March 8th. "This is the best time," said MacMillan of trade prospects. "Some teams are in the luxurious position of needing one player that could put them in a position to win the Stanley Cup."

Mark Everson of the *Post* urged MacMillan to trade Chico Resch. "He's 34 years old," said Everson, "and by the time the Devils make the playoffs, he'll probably have retired."

MacMillan admitted that he might consider dealing his veteran goalie—if a good deal came along.

None did. The deadline came and went with Resch remaining in New Jersey. His average had ballooned to 3.94 and his win-lost record was 13–34–12. "I can't blame Chico," said MacMillan. "The glaring

Tapio Levo registered four assists in first game back from Finland, then continued to lead the team in scoring.

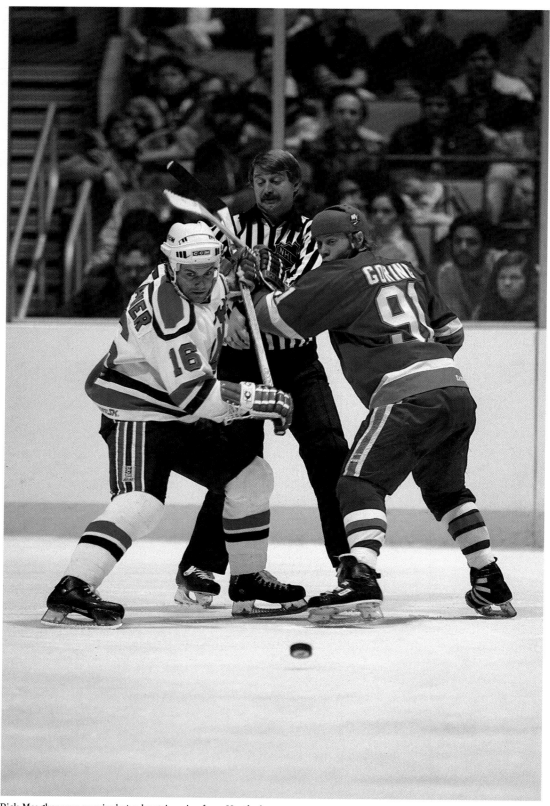

Rick Meagher was acquired at a bargain price from Hartford.

Chico Resch was destined to be the Devils' focal point throughout the early years at The Meadowlands.

The "Kid Line" of Paul Gagne, Aaron Broten (wearing #24 before switching to #10) and Jeff Larmer was one of the bright spots in '82-83.

weakness on our club is that we often give up the blue line and back into Chico."

Before the season ended, Resch redeemed himself handsomely. On March 21st, at Byrne, he stymied the Rangers for a 4–2 victory. It tied the season series at three wins apiece and thrilled the audience of 19,023 who filled the arena. "I give the Devils a lot of credit," said Rangers coach Herb Brooks. "They came up big when they had to."

The Rangers had rallied from a 0–2 deficit to tie the score 2–2 in the second before Aaron Broten twice beat Glen Hanlon in the third period to seal the victory. "The Battle of the Hudson is all we got left,"

chirped MacMillan, "and now it's all evened up."

On March 25th the Devils played spoiler again, squeezing a 6–5 win over the Flyers, and finished the season (17–49–14) with a measure of respect by beating out Pittsburgh by three points for fifth place.

"The Devils are going to be contenders in a few years," predicted Flyers coach Bob McCammon. "That's a pretty spirited hockey club going in the right direction."

MacMillan was hopeful that the flight pattern would move them considerably higher—if not into a playoff berth—in 1983-84, their second season at The Meadowlands.

4

AT WAR WITH WAYNE GRETZKY

It isn't often that one incident could shape a season but that is precisely what happened to the Devils in 1983-84. Incredibly, the episode didn't even take place on the ice but rather in the enemy dressing room one November night at Northlands Coliseum.

Under Billy MacMillan's stewardship as general manager and coach, the Devils sputtered to a more dismaying start in October 1983 than they had in the previous autumn, their first in New Jersey.

Unquestionably, hopes had been loftier the second time around. "We made strides last year," said MacMillan, "and I'm hopeful we'll make even more this year."

Bang! Bang! Right off the stick, the Devils took a one-two punch from the Rangers, losing at Madison Square Garden in the season's opener, October 5, 1983, 6–2 and then going down to the Blueshirts again at Byrne two nights later, 3–1.

There was little to commend. New York scored three shorthanded goals at the Garden and at Byrne the Devils went 0–9 on the power play.

A 6–3 victory at Detroit offered some solace with Ron Low recording the win in the nets for New Jersey. MacMillan shepherded his players home for an October 14th match against Quebec.

The game against *Les Nordiques* could have gone either way and, heaven knows, what would have happened if the Devils had tied or even won. But it was 4–4 with less than two minutes remaining in the third period when Quebec got the winner and then added an empty net goal for a 6–4 conclusion.

Then, the season crumbled around Mac-Millan. His club proceeded to lose to Toronto, Chicago, Vancouver, Los Angeles, Washington, the Islanders, Pittsburgh, Hartford, and the Islanders again. Ten consecutive losses. The club's record after 13 games was 1–12–0! The power play shutout

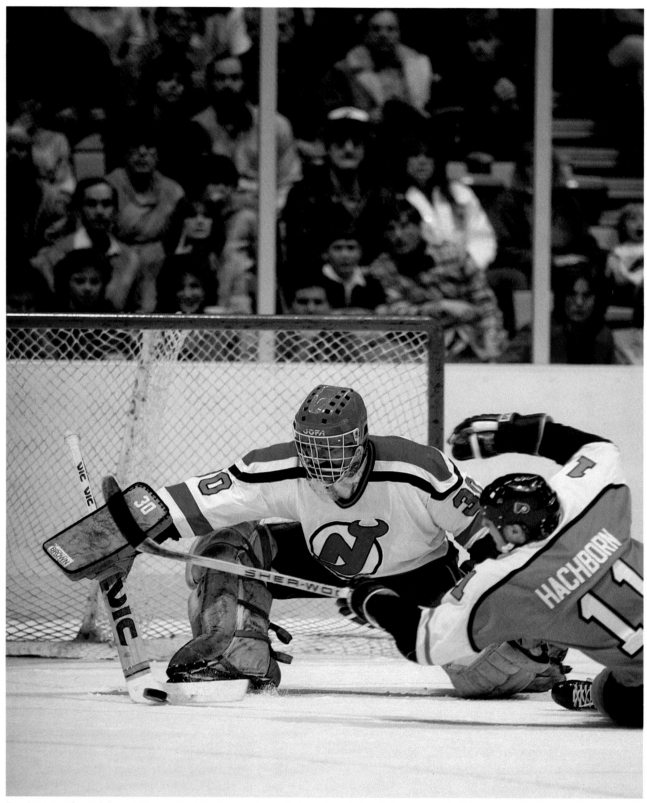

Ron Low, popular and dependable as Chico's backup, inadvertantly helped spark Gretzky's comments in Edmonton.

AT WAR WITH WAYNE GRETZKY

streak was 30. And adding injury to insult, Ken Daneyko went down with a broken right leg.

Mercifully, the losing skein was halted on November 6th when Chico Resch outgoaled Chicago's Tony Esposito, making 43 saves out of 46 shots. Six different Devils scored in the 6–3 victory.

Was this a turnaround or an illusion? The November 8th invasion of the Rangers would offer a good barometer. This time the Devils stayed close into the third period, trailing 0–2 when the Rangers broke it open with three straight goals. The game ended 5–1 for the visitors.

Again the Devils skated into an avalanche of defeats: Toronto, Calgary, Minnesota, Calgary. Five losses in a row; 15 out of the last 16 games. And now it was November 19, 1983. With a 2–17–0 record — four points in 19 games — MacMillan's troops limped into Northlands Coliseum.

Ron Low started in goal for New Jersey. He was well known to Edmonton fans and players, having tended goal for the Oilers over four seasons before being traded to New Jersey in 1983. While not a spectacular netminder, Low was a favorite with just about everyone even in a visiting uniform.

"We had pretty strong ties," said Edmonton defenseman Kevin Lowe, "because Ronnie had been a part of our team when we were just beginning to jell. He was one guy you always could talk to no matter what uniform he was wearing."

Much as they liked Low, the Oilers were merciless in their treatment of him that evening. They pumped eight goals past him through two periods of play and were so overwhelming that MacMillan felt obligated to pull his starter and replace Ron with Resch for the third period.

The Devils kept the score respectable until the final ten minutes when Edmonton players reacted like piranhas to a wounded deer. They swarmed around Resch and riddled him with five goals in the last half of the period. The final tally was 13–4, representing the largest score ever run up against the franchise.

And the swarming was not over yet.

Reporters descended on the Oilers' dressing room for comments, especially from Wayne Gretzky, who had eight points on three goals and five assists. By this point in time, The Great One had become THE premiere personality in hockey and his words carried extra weight when he delivered a peroration.

On this night he had plenty to say.

Prodded with leading questions from the newsmen, the still naive Gretzky was lured into a denunciation that he would have avoided, had he had the luxury of replay. But he answered spontaneously when queried about the bombardment of his buddy Low.

"It got to a point where it wasn't even funny," said Gretzky. "how long has it been for them? Three years? Five? Seven? Probably closer to nine. Well, it's time they got their act together. They're ruining the whole league.

"They had better stop running a Mickey Mouse operation and put somebody on ice. It's not a question of not working. It's a question of talent. I feel sorry for Ronnie and New Jersey. The 37 shots we took were all good shots. They struggled in Kansas City, they were awful in Colorado and now look what is happening."

There was a lull before the backdraft blew out the media doors. The 13–4 game took place on a Saturday night in Edmonton, after most of the New Jersey-New York newspapers had their last editions put to bed. Little other than the scoring results appeared in most Sunday papers, but by Monday the headlines were blaring all over the country. GRETZKY TAKES SLAP AT

Billy MacMillan was out . . .

AT WAR WITH WAYNE GRETZKY

. . . Tom McVie was in on November 22.

DEVILS ORGANIZATION barked the headline in *USA Today*. The New York *Post* was more direct. GRETZKY: DEVILS ARE MICKEY MOUSE TEAM.

The Mickey Mouse theme began snowballing. To his surprise, Gretzky began feeling the heat and experiencing considerable remorse the more he considered his intemperate putdown. What surprised him was the groundswell of public opinion AGAINST his tirade.

"You'd have thought I'd criticized Miss Newark or something," said Gretzky. "The fans went crazy against me. In retrospect, I probably shouldn't have said it, but I was feeling so bad about the way we'd killed them and I liked some of their guys, Ronnie Low and Chico Resch. I made the mistake of trying to divert the blame from those guys, but maybe it wasn't my place to lay blame or divert it."

Dr. McMullen and the Devils high command were suitably disappointed in the Gretzky filibuster and registered their protest. Nevertheless, the words had been spoken and, by repetition, gained currency. It is the law of sensational journalism. If you have a good angle, ride it, ride it, ride it, until the opposition drops it first.

Knowing this was small solace for MacMillan. With a 2–18–0 record, four points in 20 games, he hardly could be expected to win kudos around the circuit. Certainly, the Mickey Mouse label was at least symbolically affixed to his regime, and he would have to pay the price for a team that lost an awesome 16 out of 17 games.

On November 22, 1983, MacMillan was dismissed as general manager and head coach. Max McNab was named G.M. and Tom McVie, who had been coaching the Maine Mariners, was promoted to head coach. In addition Marshall Johnston was reassigned to director of player personnel, replacing Bert Marshall.

At first the change had a salutory effect. Over a seven-game spread under McVie the Devils actually won three, lost three, and

The fans' emotions ran high . . .

tied one. In the next five game span they were 2–2–1. Not bad.

Then, McVie discovered what is was like to be Billy MacMillan. Between December 20 and January 4, the Devils dropped seven in a row. However, they then did what they couldn't do for the previous coach; they recovered and put together three more victories in five games.

All of this was merely a prelude for what fans have been anticipating for almost two months; a visit by Gretzky & Co. to The Meadowlands. On Sunday, January 15th, the Oilers would confront New Jersey for the first time since The Great One uttered his deathless Mickey Mouse slur.

One might have thought a Stanley Cup final was unfolding at Byrne. Certainly, this was a major media event as newsmen,

television crews, radio broadcasters, and feature writers descended on East Rutherford. And if ever a team scored a pyrrhic victory in defeat, the Devils did just that.

But before the game even started, Gretzky scanned the stands and understood what he had done. Fans were wearing Mickey Mouse ears and carrying signs, GRETZKY IS GOOFY.

"Before the game," said Oilers general manager-coach Glen Sather, "Wayne was nervous because of the comments he had made. But the fans were good. They didn't overreact. In fact, I would like to see more fun poked at the whole thing. I mean, they could have had Annette Funicello sing the National Anthem."

One of the most arresting signs was carried by three teenaged girls who displayed it above the plexiglass in the Oilers end during the pre-game warmup. GLEN SATHER PRESENTS GRETZKY AND THE MOUSE-KATEERS.

Nonplussed, the Oilers jumped from the opening face-off and took a 5–2 lead into the third period. Was this to be a repeat of the Edmonton embarassment?

No way. Within the first 4:15 of the third period, the Devils stormed Andy Moog's barricades and put two past the Oilers goaltender. The capacity crowd of 19,023 was going bananas, shrieking for the tying goal. The home club poured volley after volley at Moog; 15 shots in all over the final 20 minutes but, darn it, could not get the equalizer.

A classic of its kind, the contest ended with a 5–4 Edmonton victory but for the Devils it was, as Edmonton *Sun* writer Dick Chubey put it, "a moral victory."

Assertive Tom McVie was ready for the questioners in the press room following the fray. "We'd like to prove to twenty other clubs that we're for real," said McVie, "and they're going to have to do everything they can to get two points from us. We'd like to show the NHL headquarters that we're definitely trying to straighten things out.

"I know it's going to be tough at times. I like to quote Waylon Jennings' song that things can't always be what you want them to be. That 'Sometimes it's Heaven. Sometimes it's Hell. And sometimes I don't even know.'"

Gretzky, who had no goals but three assists, was contrite. Clearly, the experience was traumatic for him. He appeared anxious about the grilling but, as always, faced up to his interrogation.

"I was feeling my way through the game," he admitted. "I regret what I said. I didn't mean to insult anyone personally or any individual. But I'm 23 years old and I made a mistake. My father, who I learned a

. . . when Gretzky next appeared at The Meadowlands.

tremendous amount from, is 43 and he'll tell you he had made mistakes. It happened and it's something I have to live with. It's over and done with."

Wayne acknowledged that some of the heat was deflected by the 4-game scoring streak he brought into the game. "If I didn't have the streak going, I think there would have been a lot more talk of ah, ah...."

Then, a pause. He was about to utter the words *Mickey Mouse* but caught them just in time. He trailed off laughing, as if to suggest that the words *Mickey Mouse* weren't about to pass his lips again; at least not when the Devils were around. "I learned one rule out of all of this," he concluded, "and that is not to criticize anyone in public."

The Devils had ten wins at the time of Edmonton's visit. They would add seven

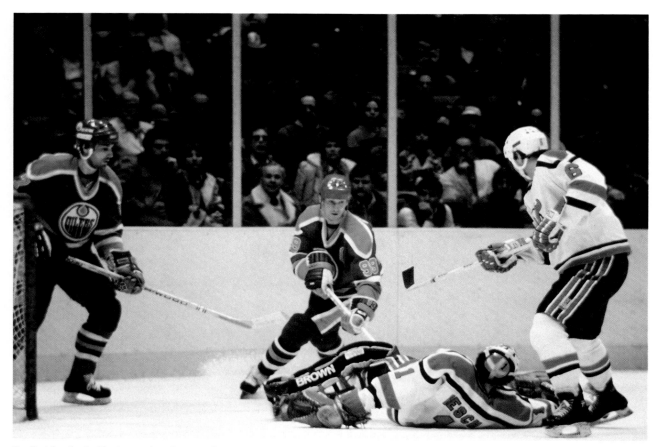

For Gretzky, the incident was a learning experience.

more between mid-January and April 1, 1984, when they concluded their campaign at home with a 3–1 loss to the Bruins. Their 17–56–7 record gave them a total of 41 points, three more than the Penguins and the right to claim fifth place once more in the Patrick Division.

This time, however, there were those who actually criticized McVie for coaxing his players to play their potential down the homestretch. Some of the cognoscenti of The Fourth Estate actually suggested that the Devils should aim for sixth place so that they would have the league's worst record and thereby qualify to draft the prodigious Mario Lemieux in the first round of the draft.

Lemieux, a hulking French-Canadian

Junior hockey ace, was reputed to be an oversized Gretzky-of-the-future and he was said to guarantee the success of any franchise lucky enough to obtain him.

McVie dismissed any suggestions that the Devils target Lemieux.

"We're here to try to win hockey games," he said. "It's the honorable thing to do."

Critical wins over Pittsburgh on March 6 and Boston on March 17 insured a fifth-place finish for New Jersey as the Penguins drowned down the stretch. Mario Lemieux would not be a Devil but honor was on McVie's side.

With the Mickey Mouse episode behind them, the Devils shook off the disappointments of 1983-84 and looked to a fresh campaign with a brand new general staff.

Jan Ludvig's career-high 22 goals in '83-84 were second only to Bridgman's 23.

Joe Cirella scored a goal and an assist in the '84 All-Star Game at The Meadowlands, raising fan expectations to an unrealistic level.

5

THE DOUG CARPENTER YEARS I

A new era in New Jersey Devils history was ushered in on May 31, 1984, when club chairman, Dr. John McMullen, announced that Doug Carpenter would be the new head coach.

To some, this was a curious choice. The 42-year-old redhead from Cornwall, Ontario, was virtually unknown except to hockey professionals and a handful of purists.

In fact, Carpenter had truly paid his dues in the ice game. The lean, sharp-featured leader had played in Montreal as a Junior Canadian, then rode the old Eastern League buses in such distant places as Greensboro, North Carolina, and Jacksonville, Florida, and eventually moved up to the realm of coaching.

During the 1979-80 season he was heading Cornwall's entry in the Quebec Junior League when George (Punch) Imlach, the legendary leader of the Toronto Maple Leafs, was scouting the Memorial Cup finals in Regina, Saskatchewan. In time Carpenter's Royals would win what is considered the Stanley Cup of Canadian Junior hockey.

"I said to myself, 'Who's the kid coaching Cornwall?'" Imlach remembered. "He did a tremendous job with a team that wasn't supposed to win, came away with all the biscuits. I liked the way he handled the team, and handled himself on the bench. I liked his system of play."

Imlach liked Carpenter so much, he hired him to coach the Leafs' farm team in Moncton in 1980-81. He did well enough to be moved on to Toronto's Cincinnati minor league club and, again, Carpenter impressed.

"We didn't give him a great deal of talent to work with, but he didn't complain," added Imlach. "Doug did the best he could with what he had."

When the Leafs put a farm club in St. Catharines, Carpenter was designated to coach the American League club and, after

In May of '84 the Doug Carpenter Era began.

two years, was ready — at least in Imlach's estimation — for the NHL. But politics, which resulted in the disposing of Imlach, intervened and Carpenter was left dangling after Punch left Toronto.

Carpenter was invited to New Jersey for interviews and immediately impressed Dr. McMullen. "I was a naval officer in World War II," the Devils' chairman said, "and one thing you learn about in the navy is people. You have to judge them and find out what they'll do in a tough spot. So when Doug came down to be interviewed, I said to myself, 'I'm gonna find out if this guy has confidence.' I told him he could work for us but that he wasn't getting a contract. When he said, 'That's okay with me,' I figured we had something."

Carpenter: "I didn't sell myself when I talked to the Devils. Sure, you say to yourself you want to present a good side. After all, you want a job. But I was just myself, no

phony stuff." Just what the Devils had would remain uncertain until Carpenter took control of the team in training camp and launched the 1984-85 campaign. In a related move, the club also named 1984 U.S. Olympic coach Lou Vairo as Doug's assistant. A native of Brooklyn, Vairo had played roller hockey on the city's streets before deciding on a coaching career. He was a veritable local boy who made good.

"Coaching in the New York Metropolitan Area," Vairo enthused, "is a dream-come-true for a fella like me."

Neither Carpenter nor Vairo suffered any illusions about their challenge. They inherited a club that had gone 17–56–7 the previous season which was seven fewer wins than the previous year. In the process the Devils went from among the youngest teams in the NHL to the oldest. The franchise now had its 12th coach in 12 seasons and the Devils third in three.

But there were some sources of optimism. Right-wing Tim Higgins, who had scored 18 goals since arriving from Chicago in January 1984 would spearhead the offense that included number one draft choice (second overall) Kirk Muller. The defense would have a new face in Canadian Olympian Bruce Driver and captain Mel Bridgman was playing some of his best hockey at center. Then, there was 1983 top draft choice John MacLean, a youngster who seemed ready for the bigs.

After watching MacLean in training camp, Carpenter opined, "At times, John has been the best player on the ice."

Goaltending seemed to be the least of the general staff's concerns. Although his 4.18 goals against average was not Vezina Trophy stuff, Chico Resch still was in his prime and had been impressive enough the previous year to play in the annual All-Star Game. Ron Low, as he had in 1983-84, would be the back-up goalie.

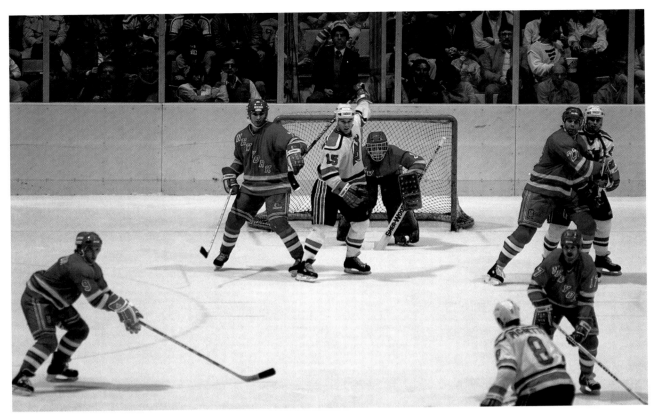
John MacLean got on-the-job training in Carpenter's first year.

Carpenter's concern was extracting more production from players such as Jan Ludvig, Paul Gagne, Aaron Broten, and Pat Verbeek. "We've got a lot of second and third players who have yet to perform up to what I believe their potential is," said Carpenter. "Guys like Ludvig, Verbeek, Broten, and Gagne should all do better than 20 goals. And I think Bridgman and Higgins can both improve on their numbers as well.

"Somehow, we have to close the 52-point gap between fourth and fifth place in our division. The Rangers, Flyers, Washington, and Islanders all will be stronger. So what do you do? That's what Lou and I are up against. We have to build a nucleus. I know what kind of battle I'm in for and what kind of work it takes. I'm a hard worker but I'm not a miracle worker."

Carpenter's debut at The Meadowlands was hardly inspiring. A crowd of 5,854 showed up for an exhibition game against Hartford on September 25, 1984, and watched the home club get beaten 3–1. If the coach was awed, he didn't show it. "It was just a hockey game," he would assert after the match. "Actually I'm very pleased with the team. Everybody is skating hard and is in good condition. It was a good camp and we came out of it with no injuries."

Certainly, nothing about training camp caused the local media to tilt toward the optimistic. In its annual pre-season preview, the New York *Post* headline read, DISMAL DEVILS GOING NOWHERE—ONLY GOAL: AVOID CELLAR.

Captain Bridgman took a different view.

After a strong 22-goal season as a rookie in '83-84, Pat Verbeek slumped to 15 goals the following year.

"We're going to fool people and be better this season. General manager Max McNab thought so too, and based his hopes on the addition of Doug Sulliman and Rich Preston to the lineup. "They certainly give us some added potential up front," said McNab. "We think we're solid in goal and have a number of defensemen who can do the job. Our worries have been in the areas of scoring goals and putting out a respectable power play.

"Doug is a good two-way player and they're pretty hard to find nowadays. And Rich is a proven NHL performer who could help us as much as the other guy (Higgins) we got from Chicago."

Carpenter's debut on the NHL firing line was neither overwhelming nor overly depressing. After three games the Devils had a 1–2–0 record and prepared to meet the Maple Leafs in Game Four at Byrne Arena. It was billed as a grudge match of sorts because Toronto had unceremoniously dumped Carpenter the previous spring, but Doug minimized his personal stake in the contest. As for his club, he noted, "We've worked hard, the enthusiasm is excellent, and the execution not that bad. But we have a long way to go."

They got a good boost by knocking off the Leafs, 4–1, with a jump start from Dave Pichette who had been acquired in the waiver draft from St. Louis. "I like to control the puck and when I have a chance I like to move in the slot," said Pichette who, along with Driver, was adding to the Devils much-needed offense.

Driver was considered a long shot to make the varsity when training camp began but played well and wound up winning a spot over Ken Daneyko, a tough kid who thought he had won a place on the big club.

"You must remember," said Carpenter, "Bruce is a little older than Kenny. And

'84-85 marked Tim Higgins best season as a Devil.

Bruce had three years in college (University of Wisconsin) and one year in the Olympics (Team Canada in the 1984 Olympics). The reason Driver is better than Daneyko is that year in the Olympics."

By the beginning of November, nobody in the NHL was asking "Doug who?" when Carpenter's name was mentioned. Even the New York *Post*, which had been so pessimistic about the club in pre-season was now chirping about the Devils. A headline in its November 2, 1984, edition said volumes: CARPENTER BUILDING WINNER IN N.J.

In Toronto, Doug's mentor was glowing. "Doug knows how to develop talent," Imlach insisted. "If they give him enough time, he'll give them a winner."

Elevated to Captain the previous year, Mel Bridgman racked up 68 goals over his first three seasons in New Jersey.

THE DOUG CARPENTER YEARS I

Always in the middle of the action, Chico had his differences with the coach.

Many — but not all — players were equally pleased with the rookie coach. "Dougie's got a nice way of getting you to do things the way he wants them done," said the veteran Resch. "He corrects you in a way that doesn't get you down. He's kind of like Al Arbour in that way. He gets you pumped up, even in practice."

Exactly a month after he uttered those words, Resch discovered a harsh side of Carpenter; one that ultimately would lead to a serious rift between player and coach. On December 1, 1984, the Devils were beaten 5–3 by Chicago at The Meadowlands. In the post-game press conference, Carpenter singled out his goaltender for criticism.

"They got only four shots in the second period and scored three goals," snapped the coach. "Maybe their guy, (Murray Bannerman) outplayed our guy (Resch)."

What caught the attention of many newsmen was the fact that this marked the second time in less than two weeks that Carpenter singled out Resch for criticism. After the Devils' 5–4 overtime loss to Minnesota on November 23, he blamed Chico for the game-winner which came on a weak shot.

Whether Resch rated the razzing was a moot point. What mattered was that the Chico-Doug contretemps became the first major player-coach "story" for the media and they jumped on it. "Chico Resch is fast becoming a convenient scapegoat for the Devils," noted The *Post's* Hugh Delano.

Carpenter might have felt considerably

more heat except that he was doing the right thing in too many other areas to be challenged. They trounced the hated Rangers 6–0 on Ron Low's shutout and accomplished a handful of important firsts.

They beat the Islanders at Nassau Coliseum, which they had never done before; they beat the Flyers at The Spectrum and the Rangers in Madison Square Garden.

A year earlier in their 28 games against the big four of their division the Devils managed only one victory. Yet now they were playing at .500 hockey — six wins, six losses, and a tie.

"The players like coming to the rink," Doug explained. "They feel good about themselves. I think that's an important first step with a struggling team. We don't have nearly the talent of the top-flight NHL teams, but we play as a unit and we hang tough."

Unquestionably, Carpenter's most meaningful victory occurred on December 17, 1984. The opponents at Byrne Arena were the Stanley Cup champion Edmonton Oilers led by the inimitable Wayne Gretzky.

The Great One's "Mickey Mouse" crack was still ringing in New Jersey fans' ears, and Wayne was greeted with a thunderclap of boos when his skates touched The Meadowlands' ice. It was expected that Gretzky & Co. would rout the Carpenter Crew but, then, an amazing thing happened; the Devils literally skated rings around the champs.

They led 3–2 in the third period when an even more astonishing thing happened. Rocky Trottier broke free and headed toward Edmonton goaltender Andy Moog. As Trottier prepared his shot, the pursuing Gretzky threw his stick at the puck. Referee Andy Van Hellemond immediately blew his whistle and awarded a penalty shot to New Jersey.

Trottier calmly took control of the disk at center ice and moved in on Moog. When he could see an opening over Moog's shoulder, Trottier lifted a forehand that sent the puck flying past the goalie. From that point on Resch held the fort and the Devils skated off with a 5–2 triumph.

No less important to the anti-Gretzky claque was the fact that the Devils had halted Wayne in his pursuit of his 1,000th NHL point. Gretzky had four of Edmonton's 21 shots and an equal number to go wide or over the net but only managed one assist and finished the game with 999 points. As for the penalty shot which he forced, Gretzky said, "I threw my stick by instinct. It wasn't very smart of me."

Surely, it helped Carpenter who more and more was moving toward center stage. "Strange things happen in hockey," he said. "Everywhere I've gone, it has been similar. I guess because I've experienced it and have been fortunate to rise to the occasion before, I can be positive. And what if we continue to do well?"

THAT was the question. What if the Devils stayed on their hot course; where would it leave them?

A playoff berth still was a distant hope because of the stiff Patrick Division competition. Yet on January 14, 1985, the Devils visited Madison Square Garden again and this time smote the Rangers 2–1. Further encouragement was provided by the 21-year-old rookie center Greg Adams who was recalled from the Maine Mariners and won 13 of 14 faceoffs against the Broadway Blueshirts.

Rangers coach Herb Brooks was one of those who commended the Jerseyites. "I like the way the Devils are playing," said Brooks. "I like their checking game. They play well without the puck and have a good cohesive flow going.

"The days are gone when you could pick up easy points against them. Those people in Jersey are doing a good job. I especially like this Kirk Muller kid. I'm impressed with his tenacity."

By mid-season there was a good news-bad news situation for Carpenter & Co. The bad news was that they were beaten 3–2 by the Islanders. The good news was that their record a year ago was 8–30–2, and now they were 13–23–4 and only six points out of a playoff berth. For the first time in their three years at The Meadowlands the Devils were not out of the NHL playoff picture at mid-season.

As Max McNab had predicted, Doug Sulliman delivered nobly, scoring 18 goals to that point along with nine assists. Muller was having a splendid rookie season and captain Mel Bridgman was coming on strong. Newcomers Pichette and Driver were coming through on defense and Resch was playing adequately in goal. Penalty killing had improved substantially and even the power play was showing signs of coming out of a two-year slump.

"From what I hear," said Carpenter, "nobody's joking about this year. I can't complain one single bit about commitment or sacrifice by any of our players."

Chico Resch: "We don't have nearly the talent of a lot of teams but, I'll tell you this, we're inching along."

But once Carpenter got his club into the final playoff drive the inching became more agonizingly slow and painful. A 5–1 clobbering by Calgary in late February dropped the Devils back into last place with only 21 games remaining. By March 1st, they had lost their sixth in a row — 4–1 to Hartford at Byrne Arena — with no light at the end of the tunnel.

This was followed by an injury to Driver and more March woes. A 6–3 loss to Winnipeg on March 12th left them 2–9–2 in their past 13 games and five points behind fourth place New York. "It's discouraging," said Resch, "but it still might work out."

In a sight which has become commonplace, Kirk Muller (wearing #27 as a rookie) and MacLean share one of their earliest post-goal celebrations.

Alas, the losses continued — 7–4 to Boston, 7–3 to the Rangers, 4–1 to Washington, 3–2 to Vancouver, 5–3 to Philadelphia, and 4–3 to Pittsburgh — until by March 27th the playoff bid was effectively nullified.

In their 80th game, at home, the Devils lost 6–1 to the Flyers. New Jersey finished in fifth place in the Patrick Division for the third straight season, with a season record 22–48–10 for 54 points.

"It was the same old script," Carpenter concluded. "We outshot them. We had the opportunities, but we just never finished them off. We must have hit the net four or five times. Still, we improved 13 points over last year and may have improved by as many as 18 or 20 if not for an eight-game losing streak. But I am disappointed that we did not make the playoffs."

Goal-scoring remained the club's weak underbelly. With 22 goals, captain Bridgman was the leading scorer (22–61–83) and Gagne led the team in pure goal-scoring with 24.

Dave Lewis, Doug Sulliman and Rich Preston injected a level of professionalism which set a high standard for the team's younger players.

On the plus side was the dramatic improvement of John MacLean as well as rookies Muller and Adams. One couldn't argue with the progress that was made.

"We made an immense amount of progress this season," Resch added. "But, yes, I think a lot more will be expected of us next season. Our record doesn't show it, but we accomplished a lot of good things this season. We found out what we're capable of doing. We were in a playoff race almost down to the end. We got tired in the second half of the season and didn't finish up well."

Added Carpenter, "We were workaholics. We didn't roll over and play dead. We established the fact that we have a good work ethic, good young players, are moving forward in the right direction. We established credibility around the league. We weren't looked at as easy pickings any more."

Carpenter followed up by taking the helm of Team Canada in the World Champion-ships at Prague and helped deliver a Silver Medal including a 3–1 triumph over the Soviet Union, Canada's first win over the Russians in either the World Champion-ships or the Olympics since 1961.

The coach's reward was a new two-year contract which was presented to him in May 1985. Doug was grateful for that but allowed that several goals sought by the club had yet to be achieved.

"Winning 22 hockey games is not beating the world down by any means," he observed. "Nothing has changed. Like I said in the fall, our offensive production has to improve."

Year I of Doug Carpenter could be considered a modest success based on the improved point total but, as the critics noted, more was expected of the team in 1985-86. Chico Resch summed up the prevailing opinion when he asserted, "Next season is going to be very pivotal for us."

6

THE DOUG CARPENTER YEARS II

Although Carpenter never publicly put his cards on the table, a number of others involved with the team realized that Doug's rookie year was not warmly received by some of the club's veterans.

As Rich Chere of the Newark *Star-Ledger* remarked, "Carpenter was greeted by a core of veteran players on the down side of their careers who might've prolonged their days in the NHL by getting the rookie coach canned early in the season. Various players and front office personnel confirm the power play clash."

A member of the 1984-85 team noted, "Doug was tough on a few guys last year but he probably had to be. Some guys thought they were the coach and you can't run a team like that. Besides, I think Doug was tougher on Lou Vairo than any of the players."

While Carpenter was enjoying the security of his new contract, he received devastating news in mid-June when it was learned that 21-year-old Pat Verbeek had severed part of his left thumb in a bizarre farm accident. Verbeek, one of New Jersey's most promising forwards, required six hours of microsurgery to repair the damaged thumb and there was considerable question about his hockey career.

"His future," said G.M. Max McNab, "is a major concern."

Of less concern was Kirk Muller. Carpenter predicted that the galvanic forward was capable of lifting his goal total from 17 as a rookie to 22 or even 25, with a break here and there. Similarly, John MacLean was viewed as a sharpshooter-in-the-rough.

In order to bolster goaltending, McNab signed free agent Alain Chevrier. That was followed by the inking of free agent Peter McNab, a veteran sharpshooter, and a deal with St. Louis in which New Jersey obtained rugged Perry Anderson for Rick Meagher. Still seeking scoring punch, the Devils obtained Mark Johnson from the

Mark Johnson added offensive spark.

goaltending job with Chevrier and young Craig Billington. "I'm equally impressed with the three goalies," said Carpenter. "That's why I kept them through training camp."

Also retained was the club's 1985 top draft choice, defenseman Craig Wolanin. "It could be two weeks, two months, or eight years," Carpenter said of the 18-year-old hulk.

The 1985-86 season officially opened for the Devils at Philadelphia's Spectrum. For the first time in franchise history, enthusiasm among even the most severe critics was the order of the day. DEVILS DESTINED FOR PLAYOFFS predicted the New York *Post*. "Don't call Bellevue," said reporter Hugh Delano. "There isn't a lunatic on the loose. The Devils CAN make the playoffs this season."

Sure enough, they rallied from a 3–0 deficit to beat the defending Wales Conference champions. If that wasn't surprise enough, New Jersey did it with Chevrier making his first NHL appearance. Alain made a total of 33 saves and played well enough to suggest that he might even bump Resch as the starting netminder. Although no one knew it at the time, this would ultimately lead to a Carpenter-Resch rift that never would be mended.

It wouldn't be the only problem Doug would have with his troops.

Doug and Jan Ludvig were less than pals and this resulted in the Czech being benched several times. Then, there was a distance that widened between the coach and his assistant, Lou Vairo. This too would be irreparable.

There were no complaints about Carpenter at the season's start. The Devils won their first three games before turning mortal on October 1, 1985.

The three victories tied the club record for consecutive wins at the start of the

Blues for Shawn Evans and, finally, defenseman Randy Velischek was picked up in the waiver draft just prior to the season opener.

DEVILS FORWARDS BRING NEW HOPE blared the New York *Times* headline on October 9th. Johnson was targeted as center for Kirk Muller and Tim Higgins while McNab was earmarked as the center for Mel Bridgman and Rich Preston.

"People are talking about us making the playoffs," noted Chico Resch. "I think we have the players to do it this year."

Resch would vie for the number one

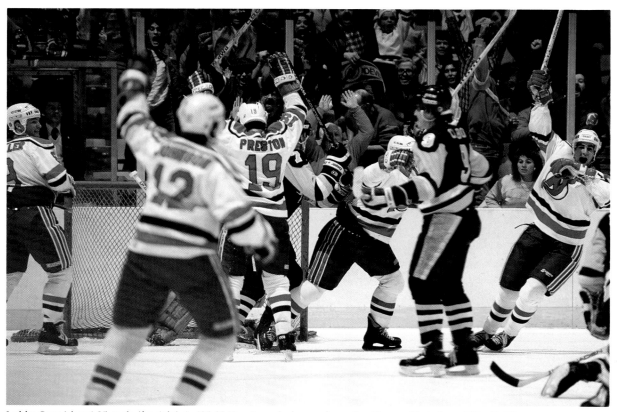

Led by Greg Adams' 35 goals (far right), in '85-86 New Jersey had seven forwards with over 20 goals, and 10 with 18 or more.

season. Critics praised the foresight of general manager Max McNab, who had received criticism for his conservative approach to building the team since taking over in 1983. Rather than look for short term help or aging, well-known players McNab chose to stick with his draft picks and wait—sometimes quite long—for them to produce.

But now everything was clicking. First round pick Kirk Muller was already a solid center, and Craig Wolanin, John MacLean, Joe Cirella and Ken Daneyko were all finding their roles on a team that was finally establishing an identity. The biggest surprise was Greg Adams, a free agent signee who was not even expected to make the parent club. After being called up briefly in 1984-85, he would lead the team in scoring in 1985-86.

With a solid if not spectacular group of maturing talent, though no legitimate superstars, the team was excited about its early success. But the streak ended in demoralizing fashion. With a 3–2 lead in the third period against Hartford, the Devils were unable to score despite several opportunites throughout the period. Worse yet, they allowed Greg Malone to tie the game with less than five minutes left.

In the overtime, the Devils' defense looked truly inept, allowing a foolish goal in less than two minutes. "It was a breakdown," agreed Carpenter.

New Jersey defenseman Bruce Driver got caught flatfooted on a 3-on-2 break, after Dave Pichette's pass was knocked down by Hartford's Scot Kleinendorst, who immediately passed the puck to teammate Ray Ferraro.

Alain Chevrier's emergence signalled a changing of the guard.

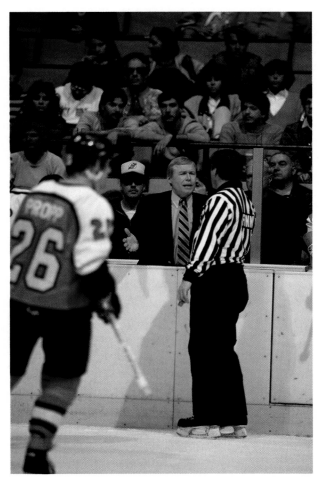

Despite problems, the team continued to progress under Carpenter.

"My first thought was to go for the intercept, but it was too late to do that," said Driver, unhappy but making no excuses. "Then I started to back up, but I was going too slow."

More frustrating yet was the fact that Resch made the initial save of the shot by Kevin Dineen, only to have the rebound bounce off Dineen's chest and into the goal. It was the wrong way to end a winning streak.

"When you let one get away — and we let this one get away — it's tough," said a terse Carpenter after the game.

That loss cannot be overemphasized in any evaluation of the Devils season. Not only was it the beginning of a long, disastrous campaign after the short-lived streak, but it also revealed a problem that talent alone could not correct: The team lacked character and thus was not even able to play up to its own potential. Nor could they bounce back from a loss, which was about to become glaringly apparent.

The Devils lost the following night in St. Louis by a score of 4–3, despite the 2nd goal of the season for Muller, who was rapidly fulfilling his potential and would be one of the few things Devils' fans had to cheer about. Though they outshot the Blues, they were 1–4 on the power play and completely inept at penalty killing, yielding 2 goals while at a disadvantage.

Two more losses followed. An abysmal 5–1 effort against the Rangers and a 6–4 loss to Chicago saw the team score only once on thirteen power play opportunities.

There were positives, to be sure. Where six months earlier it had been feared that Pat Verbeek's career was over, now the gutsy 21-year-old right wing was back at his post scoring goals as if nothing ever happened to his thumb.

"It really hasn't bothered me," said Verbeek. "The only thing is I only have feeling

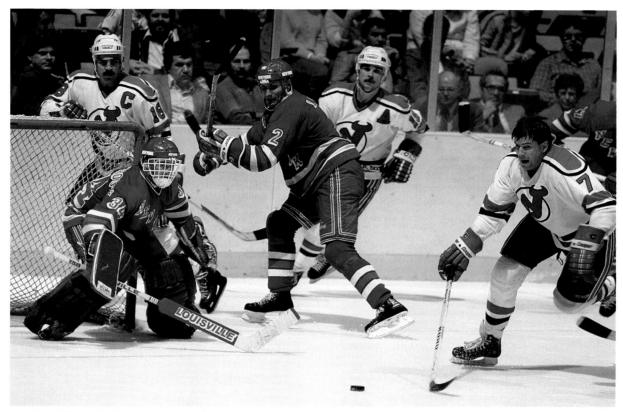

The "Fossil Line" of Bridgman, Preston and Peter McNab (L-R) had a last hurrah as the kids began to take over.

down to the joint. I can't feel the stick from the joint to the end of the thumb. I have to squeeze tight so the stick doesn't fall out of my hand. That's happened a couple of times. In a couple of years reporters will forget the incident ever happened."

Unfortunately, a pattern that would bedevil the Carpenter years was developing. A delicious taste of winning hockey at the season's start would give way to a bitter aftertaste of losing at a time when the club would have been sweetening its playoff position. In 1985-86 it would be an eight-game non-winning streak that would begin in mid-December and not end until the Devils eked out a 8–7 win over the Black-hawks in Chicago Stadium as Doug Sulli-man scored the decisive goal at 12:17 of the third period.

The mid-season report was not encour-aging. The Devils on January 24, 1986, were 14–25–1, 7–11–1 at home and 7–14–0 on the road. They were 5–15 for the second quarter, 2–7 at home and 3–8 on the road.

The pivotal game to this point was a 4–1 loss to the Rangers at a time when they could have snared fourth place. They had since plunged to last place, ten points behind the Manhattan sextet and owned the third lowest point total in the league.

Offense simply was too inconsistent to be effective, and the defense lacked toughness until Ken Daneyko was recalled from Maine on January 2nd. Greg Adams was the club's best goal-scorer with 17 red lights after 40 games. More and more, the 37-year-old Resch was the target of Carpenter's wrath, although some insiders suggested that Car-penter resented Resch's impact on the team and attempted to weaken his influence on

MacLean scored 21 goals in '85-86 and has never looked back.

the younger players, over whom Carpenter wielded the most power. The feud finally was settled when Resch was traded to the Flyers hours before the March trade deadline. In reality, after all Resch had meant to the team, the trade would not have been made if Chico had not conversed with team owner McMullen and agreed to move onto the contending Flyers. Carpenter's competition had been removed but whether he could mold the team into a contender still was an open question.

While one hero, Resch, departed, another was developing a block of fans in New Jersey. By late February 1986 Ken Daneyko had established himself as the most robust hitter among the blueline corps. In a 7–2 Devils victory over the Islanders, Daneyko used his bulk to his advantage moving Bryan Trottier, Mike Bossy, Brent and Duane Sutter out of the goal mouth. Besides, his centering pass set up Doug Sulliman's go-ahead goal late in the second period.

"I can take the odd chance now," said Daneyko, "because I feel comfortable out there. My game is to play defensive, but I feel I can contribute offensively. I know I have to play a physical game because we don't have the biggest club."

With Resch gone, the goaltending burden rested with Chevrier, who treated his rookie campaign as a learning experience. "He's aggressive but smarter," said Carpenter. "He's found out how you play nets in the National Hockey League which he didn't know at the start. He's learned to play within his limitations as well as to communicate with his defensemen, when to come out and when not to come out and the tendencies of certain players in the league."

Chevrier employed the traditional, stand-up style favored by Hall of Famers Bernie Parent and Ken Dryden. His problem was that he tended to gamble a bit too much in a league where a goalie can get burned when he roams from his crease.

"I'm still going out all over the place," said Chevrier in the final month of the campaign, "but I'm more controlled. I'm still aggressive but I can't be over-aggressive."

Any chance for a playoff berth was dissipated between March 9-19 when the club became mired in a six-game losing streak and once again they finished as also-rans.

Lady Luck certainly did not smile benignly on the Jersey skaters. Dave Pichette, who had been counted on to anchor the point on the power play suffered a concussion on January 8th and eventually was traded. Tim Higgins, who was supposed to be an offensive force, scored only nine goals. (He was traded in the off-season for Claude Loiselle.) Paul Gagne, another for whom hopes were high, scored in his first five games of the season against Philadelphia—and seven of his first ten against the Flyers—but could score against precious few other teams.

Still, there were elements of hope. The

offense moved from 20th overall in the league the previous season up to 15th in 1985-86. What's more, captain Mel Bridgman was a genuine team leader, a mainstay on the penalty-killing squad and scored 23 goals, 40 assists, and 63 points. Greg Adams' 35 goals became the most ever scored by a single player since the franchise became the Devils.

No less encouraging was the play of John MacLean who scored 21 goals and looked as if he would progress steadily while Verbeek rebounded from his injury with a respectable 25 goals and Muller continued his inspirational Bobby Clarke-style play.

Carpenter's job was not in jeopardy, despite the missed playoff. The 1985-86 Devils established franchise records with most points earned on the road in a season (23), for most wins (28) and most road wins (11). They put together the club's longest winning streak at home—four wins—but they ultimately shot themselves in the foot with the franchise record of nine consecutive losses at home. The month of January (2-11-1) did them in.

It was back to the drawing board in the hopes of finding the right stuff for 1986-87. "The truth is," noted one hockey postseason magazine analysis, "there is every reason to believe that the Devils will finally begin to accumulate more positives than negatives within a year or two, at least."

More and more, however, the onus was falling on Carpenter. No longer could the coach use his inexperience as a crutch or the fact that veteran players were sabotaging his system. Not only was the forthright Resch gone but so, too, was Doug's popular assistant, Lou Vairo, who quietly fumed over the manner in which he was treated by Carpenter and resigned at season's end.

Carpenter placed his own men, Ron Smith and Bob Hoffmeyer, in assistant

Rookie Craig Wolanin . . .

. . . and happy-go-lucky Uli Hiemer symbolized a defense in transition.

By now Paul Gagne was overshadowed in the Devils' offensive picture.

coaching roles. THERE'S NO DOUBT ABOUT IT, announced a headline in the Newark *Star-Ledger*, DEVILS ARE CARPENTER'S TEAM.

Likewise, there were some who actually believed that 1986-87 would be Carpenter's year. After 30 games of the new campaign whispers were heard that Doug has a shot at winning The Adams Trophy as coach-of-the-year.

The reason was there in black and white under the heading NHL Standings. There was New Jersey in the thick of the Patrick Division race and actually playing .500 hockey. They had just beaten the Stanley Cup champions to reach the .500 level, but Carpenter managed to keep things in perspective.

"We're not really satisfied," said the coach whose horizons had suddenly widened beyond belief. "I'll be satisfied when we're in first place. Even then I won't be fully satisfied until we win the whole thing. Then, I'll be happy and content for two weeks."

For more than two months the Devils performed like a legitimate playoff contender, no ifs, ands or buts. This, however, was not enough to satisfy the skeptics. They recalled other early-season spurts and were quick to note that, somehow, the Devils would collapse in January and forever lose their momentum.

So it was in January 1987. By late December the Devils had moved into a tie for third place in the Patrick Division just

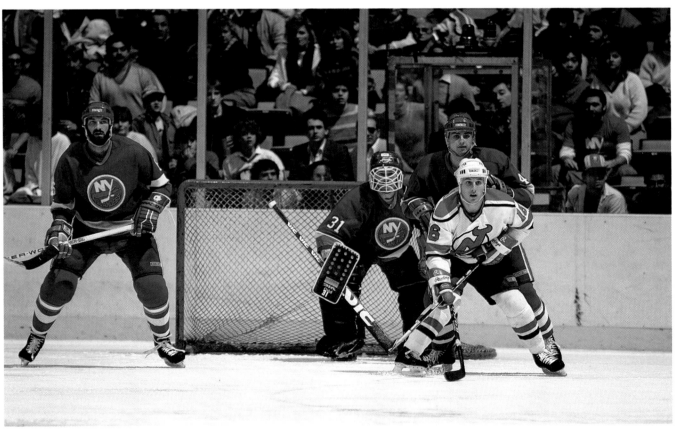

As '85-86 gave way to '86-87 all doubts about Verbeek had been erased.

Claude Loiselle fit neatly into the lineup.

two points behind the Islanders and six ahead of the Rangers. But a fortnight later, the ghosts of slumps past were haunting them. They had gone winless in seven games, dropped to fifth behind the resurgent Rangers.

There were to be no playoffs in 1986-87 either. Their record in March-April, when last-minute ground could be gained, was 5–13–1. An offbeat yet interesting record told another story about staying power. In back-to-back games they were 7–9–0 on the first night but 2–3 on the second night, raising questions about the quality of the conditioning they got.

Once again positives surfaced to soften the non-playoff blow. The Devils established club records for most points in a season with 64; most wins in a season, with 29; most home wins in a season, with 20; most shots at home, with 1,218; and fewest defeats in a season, with 45. They also had the longest unbeaten streak at home, with 4–0–1.

Aaron Broten, who was a sixth-round pick in 1980, hit a career high with 26 goals and 79 points. He was one of only two Devils to play in all 80 games. Kirk Muller also hit a career high with 26 goals and 76 points. Once considered a disappointment, John MacLean had his career high of 31 goals while Pat Verbeek tied a team mark with 35 goals.

Claude Loiselle, obtained for Tim Higgins, was a big surprise on left wing, a good defensive player who was willing to mix it up and try an offensive role, too. In the same category was Andy Brickley, leading the Devils with three shorthanded goals and doing some nice checking.

The loss of Resch did not significantly hurt New Jersey. Alain Chevrier and Craig Billington showed flashes of excellent goaltending, although Chevrier flagged as the season ground on and he completed a total of 58 games. Billington was quick and cocky and improved over the season.

While other, more impetuous club owners might have sacked their coach for failing to make the playoffs for the third straight year, Dr. McMullen refused to use Carpenter as a scapegoat. "What's happening," analyzed the coach, "is management and the coaching staff are maturing at the same time as our players are maturing. The team is starting to be put together with real Devils people. The challenges are there and we have to rise up to them.

"The ultimate goal is to make the playoffs and get a shot at the Stanley Cup. You can't be satisfied with a season where you didn't make the playoffs."

After club president Bob Butera resigned on April 24, 1987, Dr. McMullen named Lou Lamoriello as his successor. For two decades Lamoriello had been the guiding force behind Providence College's hockey success and coached the Friars for 15 years beginning with the 1968-69 season. He had ascended to the post of athletic director at Providence in 1982 and became commissioner of Hockey East in 1983.

"In Lou Lamoriello," said Dr. McMullen, "the Devils have a hockey man who had earned great respect for his accomplishments at and away from the rink, and for both his hockey and business acumen. I look forward to working with Lou as we take the Devils franchise through the next steps of our development — the playoffs and the Stanley Cup."

Lamoriello, a 1963 graduate of Providence, guided the Friars to an impressive winning percentage (248–179–13) and ten post-season tournaments in his 15 years behind the bench, including a 1983 NCAA Final Four appearance in his final season. A year after becoming athletic director, he was one of five founders of the Hockey East Association. He was selected by his peers to serve as commissioner of the seven-team league which, under his direction, has become one of the most prestigious hockey conferences in the country.

"Since the establishment of the NHL franchise in New Jersey," said Lamoriello, "the Devils have always impressed me with strong ownership and unlimited potential. After meeting and getting to know Dr. McMullen, I am convinced of this, as well as Dr. McMullen's commitment to winning in a first-class manner."

Lamoriello, who also assumed the general managership when Max McNab was promoted to executive vice-president, promptly put his imprimatur on the club. He dealt little-used Jan Ludvig to the Buffalo Sabres for powerful Jim Korn, a player Lamoriello had coached while at Providence.

At the June draft, he selected 6–3, 206 pound forward Brendan Shanahan in the first round.

"We want to get respect from other

The '86-87 team would be the last group of Devils to walk off the ice as non-contenders.

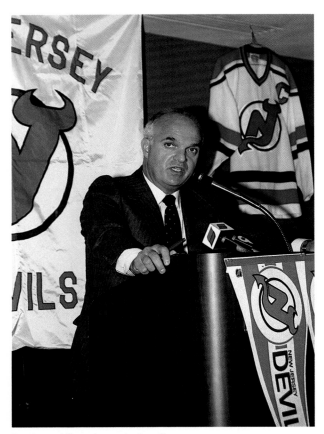
Lou Lamoriello took over in the off-season.

he took over the post, he immediately dispatched the team's leading scorer, Greg Adams, and popular goalie Kirk McLean to Vancouver for center Patrik Sundstrom and a fourth round draft choice. Over each of the past five seasons, Sundstrom had averaged 25 goals. This fact did not appease the ire of New Jersey fans who thought Adams untouchable after his outstanding rookie year (35–42–77).

"We have to do something to get to the playoffs," stated Lamoriello bluntly. "Everything we've done is to make the playoffs. Sundstrom is a quality player and we had to give up quality to get him."

Lamoriello was not one to miss the significance of losing Adams. Quite the contrary, his decision to deal the high-scoring forward was influenced by his evaluation of first-round draft pick Brendan Shanahan. Lamoriello saw talent in the youngster, who would eventually justify the G.M.'s confidence with his high-scoring, hard-hitting play.

His willingness to make such a sudden trade left many people wondering if the Devils front office was now a one-man show, but Lamoriello tactfully avoided the accusation. "Mr. McMullen has given me the authority to do things," said Lamoriello, who was certainly exercising that authority. But he hastened to add, "You won't see me make any decisions on my own. If you don't consult, you're not a good administrator. I will be relying on Max more than ever."

But would Lamoriello, Max (McNab), and McMullen be relying on coach Carpenter, who had by now become a fixture in the Devils brief history? Pre-season rumors were already circulating that Lamoriello would want his own man behind the bench. Whether the new G.M. was relying on Max or not, he handled the question of whether he would replace the coach on his own.

teams by having some players who will play a physical role, so our skill players won't be intimidated," said Lamoriello. "We want an aggressive team. If that helps us fill seats, good."

Lamoriello gave Carpenter the best team Doug had in his four starts as a coach and, for a time, it appeared that The Redhead had finally found the winning formula. New Jersey burst from the post at a gallop and raced merrily into early December looking every bit a Patrick Division powerhouse. This early success was largely a result of the daring shown by Lamoriello in the position of general manager, the traditional hot seat of the front office. The Devils' change from cellar dwellers to playoff contenders rightfully begins with the arrival of the new G.M.

The confidence of the new G.M. was amply demonstrated when, on the same day

Patrik Sundstrom would make an immediate impact in New Jersey.

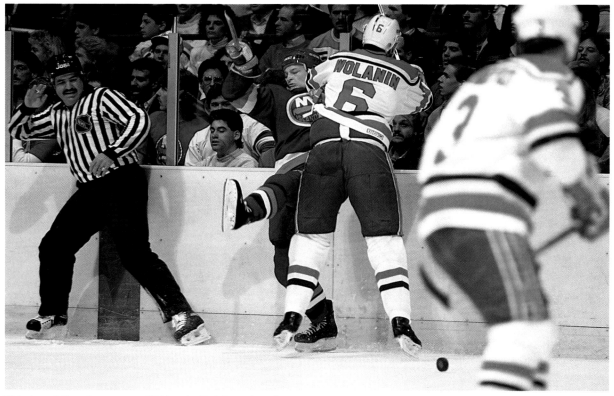

Wolanin and Daneyko were now "Taking the Body" consistently.

Said Lamoriello, "I have no such plans."

For quite some time, he had no reason to even consider it. The Devils managed to begin the season with a flourish, as they had the year before. They won the opener against Pittsburgh, 6–3, at the Meadowlands, with Chevrier stopping 29 shots. By now, Lamoriello's presence seemed to permeate all areas of the team. Defenseman Randy Velischek commented on his improved relationship with Carpenter. "The communication with Doug had been better, and the atmosphere is a little different," he said. "Everyone needs a pat on the back now and then—I think that comes from Lou."

After a 6–2 loss in Toronto, the Devils won eight of their next eleven, and were tied for first place through the end of October and into November. More important, the defense, which had been miserable in '86-87 and throughout training camp, was actually a strong point for New Jersey.

"I like the combinations we have," said Carpenter, referring especially to the Joe Cirella-Bruce Driver and Ken Daneyko-Craig Wolanin tandems. "They stay together better, have better discipline, and have cut down on giveaways in our zone."

Chevrier, who had recorded the league's worst goals against the year before, thanks to frequent barrages of 40 or more shots, was especially relieved. "I believe our defensemen are jelling into a good unit," he said, obviously pleased to see his goals against average fixed at 2.72 after eight starts. They're clearing people out in front of the net and letting me see the puck better."

Shanahan struggled, grabbing headlines only when he and John MacLean attempted to climb into the stands in Pittsburgh on October 21 to attack fans who had pelted the duo with beer. The pair were fined and suspended, yet even this admittedly foolish behavior was a sign of the Devils' overall emotion. It is significant that they managed to win the game, 5–4, displaying poise even in a chaotic situation. As rookie Doug Brown noted later, "This team has character."

That character would be tested as the Devils became targets of renewed aggression, thanks to their success and high standing in the always brutal Patrick Division.

A disheartening blow was the loss of both defenseman Tom Kurvers and power-play specialist Mark Johnson, who went down with injuries during a violent 3–3 tie with the Flyers at Philadelphia Spectrum. Those injuries would, a few games later, figure prominently in determining Lamoriello's course of action in the 2nd half.

Even without Shanahan and MacLean, who were serving their suspensions, and the injured Kurvers and Johnson, the Devils dismantled the Blackhawks on November 20, raising their league home record to 10–0–1. But seven of the next eight games would be on the road, where the team was 2–4–2. "If you are going to be a good team, you must show you can win on the road, too," asserted newcomer Sundstrom.

Confidence was high. "We'll win on the road, you can bet on it," affirmed Driver.

It wasn't a good bet. In Montreal and Calgary, the Devils lost two in a row for the first time all season, including a 9–2 beating from the Flames, easily New Jersey's worst loss of the season.

But nobody was very alarmed—at least not yet. In Edmonton the next day, Doug Carpenter was still singing his team's praises in the Edmonton *Sun*, describing their long, hard battle to respectability. "A baby needs time to mature," he said. "It's no different building a hockey team from scratch. It requires a certain amount of time to develop."

Ironically, Carpenter made these remarks at a time when the Devils were beginning a slide that would eventually lead to his dismissal. Carpenter's Devils were known for mid-season slumps, but this one occurred in the midst of the team's most successful campaign ever.

In the next loss, a 4–2 effort against Vancouver, the Devils scored only once on seven power-play opportunities. John MacLean was slumping as well, not having scored a goal in eight games. Despite his personal success, Muller was sullen. "We're disappointed in our performance," he said.

When the Devils lost a humiliating 5–1 decision to Calgary on their home ice, where they had been nearly invincible, it was obvious that the team was in serious trouble. "We played awful," said Daneyko, "and they buried us."

This time, the power play was 0 for 7, an all-time worst. "No comment on that one," said Sauve, who faced 35 shots and was the victim of a three-on-one rush which occurred, amazingly enough, when the Devils were on one of their inept power plays.

Though they still held second place, the loss to the Flames was followed by another disheartening defeat , 5–3, to the Islanders.

And then, IT happened.

On December 16th the Devils invaded Madison Square Garden. Television news crews accompanied the usual print media horde for what some observers believed would be the litmus test for the Jersey sextet. If Carpenter could fashion a win over New York, it would fortify the feeling that once and for all the Devils were playoff-bound. Even if it were a close encounter — not even a win — there would be room for optimism. However, if the Rangers burst Carpenter's bubble it would be, in the deathless words of Yogi Berra, "déjà-vu all over again."

Unfortunately, it was the latter — by a lot.

In a match that was as clear-cut as a pastrami sandwich at The Carnegie Delicatessen, the Devils were demolished. The final score, 9–3, was indicative of the play and a half-hour after the final buzzer, Carpenter seemed to be both dazed and melancholy about the events that had transpired on the ice. "We stunk," he said. "It has to be turned around."

Perhaps the loss to the Rangers was an aberration. Conceivably, the Devils would immediately get it out of their system and kick themselves into high gear once again.

Certainly, the result would determine the future, short or long term, of Doug Carpenter.

As Schoenfeld took over, a "Never Say Die" attitude was instilled.

7

THE LAMORIELLO ERA

Carpenter could not close the floodgates in time, certainly not sufficiently to persuade Lamoriello that Doug had the personal chemistry at this point in time to bring the Devils back to playoff-competitive level.

Conceivably, the president-general manager could have sat on his hands and waited out the season, thereby having a better excuse for dropping Carpenter after four straight years of missing the post-season ring. A choice was presented in late January, and Lamoriello decided that an assertive move had to be made.

He realized that neither the press nor the public might approve of his decision but he was willing to take his chances and unhesitatingly acted. In time it would prove to be a most fortuitous move.

On January 26, 1988, the media was summoned to the Arena's Winners Club where Lamoriello made the critical announcement; Carpenter would be replaced by Jim Schoenfeld.

The official announcement noted that Carpenter was relieved after three and one-half seasons behind the bench "in the wake of the five-game losing streak and 3–9–1 slide that has dropped the Devils into fifth place in the Patrick Division."

The factors for Doug's dismissal were many, but the bottom line was that his clubs invariably faltered in the critical period of January and, certainly, the evidence was all there, traceable back to the one-sided defeat at Madison Square Garden before Christmas and five consecutive losses in January.

"While I certainly respect the work Doug has done to move the team into playoff contention, I reached the conclusion that a change in our coaching staff was necessary at this time to get the Devils into the playoffs," said Lamoriello. "This is not a decision reached easily, nor is it one implemented without some regret because I do recognize the contribution Doug has made to this franchise.

"But in this business difficult decisions must be made regardless of personal feelings for the good of the franchise. At this time it is my belief that the talent on the Devils is good enough to make the playoffs and that Jim Schoenfeld will coach this team into the playoffs."

The 35-year-old Schoenfeld, a redhead like Carpenter, had coached the Buffalo Sabres to a .500 record during the 1985-86 season following a 13-year NHL career on defense, spent mostly with the Sabres.

"I'm very proud to have been offered this opportunity," said Schoenfeld, "and am very optimistic for the future."

In assessing the turnover, North Jersey *Herald News* columnist Steve Adamek observed, "Carpenter, ultimately, is the victim of the expectations he created. In other words, the Devils believed Carpenter could not reap what he had sown. They believe Schoenfeld can."

Assessing Carpenter's tenure, one must start with his record of 100–166–24 and no playoff berths. He nurtured several young players to maturity, particularly Kirk Muller who had become captain and was very effective over periods of time but not the long haul. One can conjecture forever whether or not he could have pulled the Devils out of their 1987-88 nose dive but there was little time to muse about that.

"Something had to be done," said Lamoriello. "I don't think we were going forward and I don't think Doug did either. And he tried everything."

Certainly, Lamoriello had given him the tools. In addition to developing top-draft choices such as Muller, MacLean, and Wolanin, the pre-season acquisition of Patrik Sundstrom from Vancouver was paying dividends. Lamoriello had also acquired defensemen Jack O'Callahan and Tom Kurvers, each of whom was a positive force on the club.

That oft-used term "chemistry"—so difficult to define yet held so vital to a team's success—was mentioned time and again at the press conference.

"There's a certain personality, a certain individual needed that can get us to where we can be or where we should be," added Lamoriello. "Jim Schoenfeld is the person I wanted."

Just how well the new Redhead would orchestrate the slumping hockey club, naturally, was uncertain. The media, as a whole, took a wait-and-see attitude.

"Hiring Jim Schoenfeld could be a good move," commented Hugh Delano in the New York *Post*, "but no one knows if Schoenfeld can coach in the NHL. If he can awaken the dozing Devils the way he struck fear in the hearts of rival forwards as a bruising defenseman, it could be enough to put them into the playoffs for the first time."

Devils players were not totally surprised by the decision. "We needed something to get us going," said Muller. "We needed a fresh atmosphere. We've got to get the aggressiveness back into our game. The big thing is that no one will be complacent now. Everyone knows what their role is and everyone knows they'll have to prove themselves all over again. If the team is not doing well, then the next move will have to be a player move."

Added Pat Verbeek, "A coaching change rejuvenates teams. It's a spark, and we need something to get us going again, to work harder than we have recently."

Neutral observers wondered which was the real Devils team that Schoenfeld was inheriting. Was it the one that went 12–1–1 in its first 14 games at home? or was it the one that had gone 2–9–0 in its last 11 games at The Meadowlands?

This much was certain; if the Jerseyites were to make a move, they had two months to do it. They were in fifth place, just five points ahead of the last-place Rangers who had a game in hand.

The immediate results were positive. In Schoenfeld's debut on January 28, 1988, the Devils beat the Penguins at The Meadowlands and went on a three-game streak, finding themselves in a third-place tie with the Islanders at the end of the month. Was it Schoenfeld? If nothing else, the club was alive and kicking.

"I coach pretty much the way I played," said Redhead II, explaining his style. "I expect honesty and desire from players."

Respected by his young players and a communicator in contrast to Carpenter, Schoenfeld began by infusing a new spirit in the clubhouse. He also worked on the players' achievement levels. "Jim stressed that although the team has improved each year, he felt that our level of improvement was not enough," said young defenseman Craig Wolanin. "He said, 'Let's make the playoffs.' We began working toward that goal."

Now the question was—did the Devils possess the talent to reach the playoff level for the first time in the club's history?

The goaltending tandem included maturing Alain Chevrier and tried-and-true veteran Bob Sauve. It was considered adequate but occasionally vulnerable when the defense was not tight.

Schoenfeld's backline comprised Wolanin, who still needed grooming, Joe Cirella, Ken Daneyko, Bruce Driver, Randy Velischek, Kurvers, and O'Callahan.

Under Carpenter, Velischek had been reduced to an insignificant role. Schoenfeld restored the intelligent hitter to active duty, and he soon became one of the club's most improved players. Cirella, who had been carrying an inordinately heavy workload, had

it slightly reduced and he responded with even better play.

The offense still looked for the big gun although it was bolstered by several individuals. Muller was the leader of the attack, a workhorse who never gave less than 100 percent, even when in the midst of a slump. Slowly but significantly, John MacLean was emerging as a clutch scorer, and another redhead, Doug Brown, turned into the club's offensive penalty-killer extraordinaire, frequently teaming up with the equally effective Claude Loiselle, who was New Jersey's face-off specialist.

Unfortunately, the team's most intimidating player, big Jim Korn, injured his shoulder and required surgery in February, which meant that he would be inactive until the beginning of April—a time when the Devils normally would be on the golf

In mid-winter . . .

. . . the celebration . . .

course. The second most intimidating player, Tasmanian Devil George McPhee suffered an early-season groin injury which would sideline him for the season and, for all intents and purposes, ended his playing career.

"The players," said Schoenfeld, "will be accountable to each other, to their coaching staff, and to the fans. I'm not going to turn it around; it'll be the players who turn it around."

But after the initial euphoria of the three-game winning streak, the Devils dropped three straight on the road—to Edmonton, Vancouver, and Boston. Chevrier, who had carried the burden of goaltending early in the campaign, appeared to be wearying.

Sauve stepped in on February 2 and stopped the bleeding with a 4–2 win over Montreal. Fourth-liner Andy Brickley scored a pair of goals including the game-winner. Sauve helped the club to a 3–2 mark over a five-game stretch that saw New Jersey move back into a fourth place tie. The capper was a 6–3 home win over the Rangers in which Brown scored two goals but—who else?—Brickley got the winner.

Just when it appeared that the Devils were back in the groove—they would play five of their next six games at home—the bottom fell out once more. Bang, bang, bang, they lost to Boston, Winnipeg, and the Rangers at Byrne before scrambling to take Minnesota, 8–6, only to lose in Washington and again to the Capitals at The Meadowlands.

The second loss to Washington, on March 2, 1988, was particularly meaningful to the home crowd. Offensive as the 6–1 defeat may have been, the home fans were treated to the long-awaited arrival of Sean Burke.

Drafted by New Jersey in 1985, Burke had starred for the Canadian Olympic team and was regarded as one of the most promising

. . . was just around the corner.

young goalies on the continent. So much had been written about him before his arrival at The Meadowlands that it was almost inevitable that he suffer a build-up to a letdown.

The tall, jut-jawed goaltender did not start against the Capitals; Chevrier had that dubious distinction and was beaten 40 seconds into the contest. By the end of the second period Chevrier had allowed four goals and Schoenfeld gave him the hook.

Burke's premiere was less than sensational. Mike Gartner victimized him on a breakaway at 3:19 and a screened shot by Kevin Hatcher beat the big guy less than three minutes later. With Washington winning by five goals, it was difficult for the Devils to develop any feelings of hope, nor did Burke suggest by his play that he could rally the club for a desperate homestretch drive.

"I'm sure a lot of people are expecting big things from me," said Burke in the dressing room after the defeat. "I'm not putting any extra pressure on myself. I want to help the team make the playoffs for the first time."

Burke's first NHL win three days later in Boston was not really that much more impressive than his debut. Nor was it readily apparent why coach Schoenfeld chose to grant Burke his first pro start in such an important game. Clearly, he was anxious to shake things up for the home stretch, and was willing to gamble on youth to make it happen.

The Devils won, 7–6, in overtime, on Andy Brickley's second goal of the game. Burke was poised throughout an admittedly sub-par effort, and demonstrated tenacity by going all the way and salvaging the victory in hostile Boston Garden.

"Monumental," cheered Schoenfeld, describing the victory. "The best thing was that a lot of times we could have quit, but we just hung in there and kept battling," the coach added. "To win was magnificent, but the way we won makes me much happier."

Schoenfeld was likely referring not only to his team's never-say-die attitude but the aggressive tactics of young David Maley, who pummeled Lyndon Byers early in the game, a victory of sorts in the always violent confines of Boston Garden. As the *Daily News* noted, Maley lifted the spirits of the team which was down 3–1 at the time, but quickly recovered.

Pretty or not, the hard-fought victory inspired the team as it did Schoenfeld, who went with Burke the following day at home against Philadelphia. Burke, who stopped 24 shots, keyed a 4–2 victory and displayed real character in rebounding immediately from the previous night's performance. Nor did it rattle him when the first goal went past him off teammate Craig Wolanin's stick.

His teammates seemed to agree. Patrik Sundstrom scored two goals to end a ten-game scoreless streak. "I was a little frustrated offensively earlier," he said. "I couldn't put any numbers on the board."

Wolanin atoned for his error and netted the game-winner, a hard blast from the point at 5:45 of the third. After the game, he said exactly what Schoenfeld liked to hear. "It doesn't matter who scores the winner," he asserted. "It's a team win."

Speaking of the team, it had just set a club record with win number 30, and the highest point total, 65, in the history of the franchise.

All of which didn't mean nearly as much as making the playoffs, a definite possibility now that the team began to play spirited hockey in front of their young goaltender. Burke knew what the Devils had to do to clinch the final playoff berth, and he said, quite simply, "Every game is important."

Especially the ones against the Rangers, whom the Devils led by one point, having knocked them out of fourth place with the win over Philadelphia. Schoenfeld started Burke, who would make his Garden debut under the worst kind of pressure. Schoenfeld's commitment to the young goalie was absolute. The Devils would either make the playoffs or not with Burke in the net.

That commitment would be tested after the devastating 7–4 loss at the Garden. The Rangers scored three goals in six minutes off Burke, who was then replaced by Chevrier. The loss dropped the Devils into a tie for fifth place with only ten games left to go.

After a much-needed three-day rest, the Devils traveled to Philadelphia to play the Flyers, who had relinquished their eight-week lock on first place when they lost to Burke on March 6. After the beating administered by the Rangers, one could wonder if it would be wise to start Burke in yet another division rival's arena.

But the Devils coach never wavered, and his faith in the youngster was well founded. Burke responded with a gritty 6–5 win, needing and getting production from his teammates. Tom Kurvers netted two and Claude Loiselle got the game winner. As he had done in his first start, Sean was more tough than skillful, refusing to cave in despite his second consecutive game of heavy bombardment.

Perhaps his worst game was against Quebec on March 17. Besides being his only loss, he looked bad enough to draw boos from the hometown fans. His teammates were no better, relinquishing a 2–0 lead and losing 4–2. "It's inexcusable," fumed Schoenfeld. "There's too much riding on this game to fall asleep. To say we're a young team, or we're maturing, is a bunch of crap," he added, refusing to embrace any excuse. "These guys are professionals."

Shanahan, the first round pick, ruined a Devils power play late in the second period when he attacked Robert Picard before a face-off. "I apologize to the team for what I did," said the struggling 19-year-old, who received a roughing penalty.

"The bad penalties plagued us all year," said Schoenfeld. "The lack of discipline can't go on if you want to succeed."

The loss dropped the Devils to dead last in the division, not only three points behind the Rangers but two behind lowly Pittsburgh. Worse yet, their next game was at the Cap Centre, where the Devils had been horribly jinxed throughout their short history. After the dismal performance against Quebec, it would have been the appropriate place for the Devils to completely fall apart.

But it was an even better place to pull off one of the most exciting victories in the team's history, marking the beginning of a wild unbeaten streak that would clinch New Jersey's first-ever playoff berth.

Still smarting from the boos at The Meadowlands, Burke may actually have been relieved to play on the road. In any case, both he and the team in front of him recovered dramatically from their defeat against Quebec. After surrendering two early goals, the young goalie became stingy, keeping the Devils in the game until the offense woke up.

Burke's patience paid off when Pat Verbeek tied the game with his second goal midway through the third period. Tying the score after 50 frustrating minutes ignited the Devils. Even penalties couldn't slow down the attack. Rookie Doug Brown and Claude Loiselle each scored shorthanded goals less than a minute apart, an amazing feat under any circumstances, for a 4–2 Devils win. It was the team's first ever at the Cap Centre and the team's rejuvenation was truly tangible.

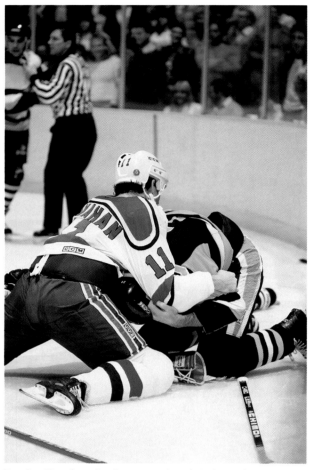

Brendan Shanahan played an aggressive role in his rookie season.

Unfortunately, at the time the victory did little for the team's place in the standings. The Devils were still last, trailing the Penguins by two points and the Rangers by five.

The next victory, an 8–2 blowout of St. Louis, left the Devils still five points behind their rivals from across the river in New York. MacLean, Cirella, and Broten each scored twice, as the offense continued what it began in the third period against Washington. Burke was solid with renewed support. The defense successfully killed five penalties. The team's remarkable roll to the playoffs had begun.

Though Schoenfeld's confidence in Burke was unquestionable, the irrefutable team effort required to pull off this unfold-ing minor miracle was amply demonstrated by the veteran Sauve. When Burke needed a rest, the coach called on Sauve, who hadn't played in three and a half weeks, to start against the Sabres in Buffalo. As the final standings would later reveal, it was a game the Devils simply could not afford to lose.

All Sauve did was make a stupendous save on Ken Priestlay's breakaway in over-time; in so doing he saved the game, and the Devils' season, when he preserved the 2–2 tie. The rest of his game was equally good. He stopped 29 shots on a night when the Devils' offense was cooled off by Buffalo, though John MacLean scored his third goal in two games, bringing his season total to 18. But for MacLean, and a rested Burke, the best was yet to come.

Burke needed the rest because his next opponent would be the Rangers, who had run him out of the net at Madison Square Garden three weeks earlier. The Devils would have the chance to pull within three of the Rangers, who held fourth place. And the game was to be played at the Meadowlands.

It was New Jersey's turn to make the Rangers look ridiculous. Less than two minutes into the first period, Muller scored the first of two goals to give the Devils an early lead. Ten minutes later, Pat Verbeek scored his first goal of the game. His sec-ond would come on a penalty shot late in the same period after the Rangers' Mark Hardy threw his stick, in desperation, at Verbeek, who was clearly controlling the puck. "The stick came out of nowhere," said Verbeek. "When the ref said it was a penalty shot my legs were shaking, like I was standing in front of class giving a speech."

Nevertheless, he scored on the chance with a deke to his left, and a backhander past Rangers goalie John Vanbiesbrouck. The sellout crowd at the Meadowlands erupted. That goal proved to be the game-winner, though Brown and Loiselle added tallies of their own. When the Rangers pulled Vanbiesbrouck, Pat Conacher scored yet another goal for New Jersey, ending the romp at 7–2. Equally impressive was the Devils' penalty killing, which stifled seven New York power plays.

"That was bigger than big for us," said Brown. "I think we deserved this."

Added Verbeek, "It's going to be a fight to the end and this team is loving it. Each game now is becoming bigger after this one."

Burke stopped 27 shots, more than vindicating his earlier disaster at the Garden. Schoenfeld was pleased. "There was a relentless effort," he said. "The players are really committed."

Having pulled within three of the Rangers and Penguins, the Devils believed in themselves as they never had before. The playoffs were within their grasp, and the stunning victory at the Meadowlands provided more than enough momentum to carry the team.

A home-and-home series with Pittsburgh made the Devils look invincible. They swept the Penguins in front of Burke, who recorded his first shutout (4–0) in the first game in New Jersey. On three occasions he stopped Mario Lemieux, the league's leading scorer, including once on a breakaway. Muller, Verbeek, and Loiselle all scored again. The Devils' captain now had 36 goals, and none of his teammates thought it coincidental that their best season also happened to be Muller's first wearing the "C" on his jersey.

After the second game in Pittsburgh, a 7–2 New Jersey victory, the team was guaranteeing a playoff berth. "We've got to win the last two games, and we're going to win them," said Verbeek, speaking through a swollen, bleeding mouth, the result of a high stick. His spirits, however, were not dampened in the least. "You can bet on it."

"Sure we can do it," echoed MacLean, who scored two goals including the game-winner, a feat he would duplicate in even more dramatic fashion a few days later.

But there was one sticking point. The Devils, still in fifth place and trailing the Rangers and Penguins by a point, had to hope the Rangers would lose at least one of their remaining games. Otherwise, even two New Jersey victories would be meaningless. "We need someone to bounce New York once," said Schoenfeld, who was forced to pull for the Jets and Quebec, the Rangers final two opponents. The Broadway Blueshirts were in Winnipeg on Friday night, April 1. The last thing the Devils wanted to see was a Ranger victory and, to that extent, their wish was granted. A goal by Paul MacLean gave Winnipeg a 6–6 tie late in the third period, sending the game into overtime. What bothered the Jerseyites was the fact that the Jets had several chances to put the game away in overtime and missed or were foiled by goalie John Vanbiesbrouck. When the contest was over the Rangers were in fourth place with a record of 35 wins, 34 losses and 10 ties for 80 points. Going into the weekend, the Devils had 78 points but two games remaining on their slate compared to one for the Rangers.

Of course, the Devils had to beat both the Islanders and Blackhawks, both difficult opponents who would make the playoffs. The Islanders were not the same team who had won four Stanley Cups in the early and mid-80s, but they were still a formidable team with a wealth of player experience and were headed for first place in the division. Both Bryan Trottier and future Hall-of-Famer Denis Potvin were still active.

But the Devils were not to be denied. They outscored the Nassaumen 5–2 with

Loiselle, Sundstrom, Verbeek, Muller, and Broten — with the game-winner — each tallying behind Burke's goaltending. That left New Jersey with a mark of 37–36–6 with 80 points and a tie with the Rangers for fourth.

This meant that if the Rangers won on Sunday night at home against Quebec — considered very likely at the time — it would give the New Yorkers 82 points and 36 wins. Thus, the Devils also had to win at Chicago, so that they could have 82 points as well but would finish with 38 victories. To break the fourth-place deadlock, the NHL gives preference to the team with more wins. Hence, the Devils would be in by beating Chicago.

The stage, therefore, was set for one of the most pulsating finishes in NHL annals.

Bob Sauve — cool under pressure when it counted most.

8

THE GAME
OF ALL GAMES

For Devils fans, the anxiety quotient could not have been higher as dawn broke on Sunday, April 3, 1988.

Their team had long ago emplaned for Chicago and its rendezvous with destiny against the Blackhawks in the 80th game of a long and memorable season.

They knew that the Rangers would face the far more vulnerable foe that night at Madison Square Garden, where the Blueshirts' match with *Les Nordiques* would start well in advance of the Windy City match.

If, as expected, the Rangers prevailed, it meant that the pressure would mount on the New Jersey heroes playing a battle-proven Blackhawks squad in one of the most hostile of all rinks for visiting teams.

But that was the luck of the draw. Who could complain. Never before had an NHL team representing Byrne Arena played so well for so long—and come so close to the coveted playoff position. And that, of course, was the excrutiating part.

As one longtime fan leaving The Meadowlands after the April 3rd Islanders game suggested, "It would be a pity, having come so far, for the boys to lose their chance on the last night of the season."

Rooters on the east side of the Hudson River couldn't care less. Their Rangers, piloted by volatile Michel Bergeron, never quite lived up to expectations. The New Yorkers believed that once they reached the playoffs, all the wrongs of the regular season would finally be righted.

"We should beat Quebec," said Bergeron. "Then, all we can do is hope the Devils don't beat Chicago."

For New Jersey, there was only one certainty; Sean Burke would start between the pipes against the Blackhawks. Heading into Game 80, Burke had compiled an extraordinary 9–1–0 record, which was amazing for any kind of goalkeeper, let alone a rookie. In plain English, the big guy was coming up BIG.

Burke's counterpart on the Rangers,

John Vanbiesbrouck, was designated by Bergeron to start the game against Quebec. The Beezer had been in and out down the stretch—in stark contrast to Burke—losing one, winning one, and tying one in his last three games. Giving up six goals against Winnipeg, however, bordered on sacrilege, and Devils followers hoped against hope that The Beezer would have one more bad game in him at the finish.

This was not to be. The visiting Nordiques skated listlessly against the Rangers and, in no time at all, it was clear that New York would cruise to a victory. John Ogrodnick opened the Rangers' scoring, and that goal proved to be the winner in a 3–0 washout of Quebec.

The beginning was brilliant for Jim Schoenfeld's troop. Ken Daneyko broke a scoreless tie at 11:07 of the second period. Instead of sitting back, the Blackhawks counterattacked with a vengeance. With big Rick Vaive screening Burke, Denis Savard slipped the puck into the far side to tie the count at 1–1. The time was 13:54 of the second period. Just 35 seconds later Dirk Graham redirected Bob Murray's right-point drive from the outside to the inside post to fool Burke for a 2–1 lead 14:29.

Adding more pain to the injured Devils was the scoreboard announcement that the Rangers had won. Still, the Jersey skaters persisted, and Pat Verbeek tied the score once more. Only eight seconds remained in the second period when "Beeker" brought TV viewers at home to the edge of their easy chairs as he knocked in the rebound of Craig Wolanin's power-play drive.

Into the third period the teams skated, tied at two until Chicago's Troy Murray blocked a Wolanin shot from the left point. Murray broke free and went one-on-one with Burke, beating him with a shot over the left glove as the ten-minute mark approached.

If Devils fans were concerned, their coach certainly did not reflect any anguish. "Heck," said Schoenfeld, "we had over ten minutes left, and I felt if we could at least tie the score, we could win it in overtime."

The high drama really took shape at 11:57 of the third period when John Mac-Lean skated in from the left side to deposit Mark Johnson's rebound where it belonged.

From that point to the end of regulation time Burke hung tough—as did Darren Pang at the Chicago end—until the buzzer signalled sudden death.

"We knew a tie would do us absolutely no good," recalled Kirk Muller, "but we also knew that we didn't want to give up a goal because a defeat would be just as bad. The trick was to play a solid game and hope for a break."

For many Devils fans, the moment of truth that night was forever etched in their memories, just as it was for New York Giants fans in 1951 when Bobby Thomson hit his playoff-winning home run off Brooklyn Dodgers pitcher Ralph Branca at Manhattan's Polo Grounds.

One such rooter tells this story:

"I was working Bill Mazer's Sunday evening sports show on Channel Five that night, and believe you me it was tough. There were a couple of Rangers fans in the studio, and we had both games going simultaneously while the game at the Garden still was on.

"A sinking feeling grew in my stomach as the Rangers widened the lead over Quebec and finally beat them. I knew the Black-hawks were going to be tough on us, and, to be perfectly honest, I didn't even think we could rally for a tie in the third period.

"Before overtime began, Mazer had to get up to the set, for his show was getting ready to go on. Hockey was going to be the main topic that night but we wanted to make sure we got the Devils' score in, even if it meant doing it in the middle of the show.

"What they did was have a runner watch the game down by the studio and then come up to tell us if anybody scored and how the game turned out.

"All I knew was that we were up there a long time and still nobody had come; which was like bad news for the Devils. I gathered that the game was going to end in a tie and the whole season would go up in smoke. But all we could do was wait—and wait."

The Devils did not wait very long once overtime began. With a little more than two minutes gone in the sudden-death, they controlled the puck in the Chicago end of the rink, but the Blackhawks recovered and appeared to be able to clear the rubber over the blue line at the left boards.

Instead, defenseman Joe Cirella managed to keep the puck inside the attacking zone and fired a drive directly at Pang.

"When Joe made that shot from the point," said John MacLean, "I was on my way to the net."

The puck richocheted off the Chicago goaltender's pads and headed for the onrushing MacLean. "My only thought at that moment," the affable Devil recalled, "was that our whole season could go down the drain if I missed. When the puck landed on my stick, I just gave it everything and somehow it went in. We were ready for the first time this season to let it all hang out."

Only minutes earlier, the Rangers, who were all watching the game in their players' lounge at Madison Square Garden, thought they had it made. After the red light flashed behind Pang, Vanbiesbrouck hung his head muttering, "I can't believe it!"

This was a phrase being echoed all over hockeydom. At Channel Five studio on Manhattan's Upper East Side, the runner had walked on to the fringe of Mazer's "Sports Extra" set with a huge piece

MacLean's goal at Chicago instantly transformed him into the Devils "Mr. Clutch." The following year he reeled off the first of three consecutive 40-goal seasons.

of cardboard and the scrawl: JOHN MacLEAN—2:21 OF OVERTIME.

"I did a double-take," remembered the Devils fan who worked the program. "It was as if I had to see the cardboard again—and again. Long afterward, I was still shaking my head. After the show, I went to the bar down the block and had two Bloody Marys."

Meanwhile, the Devils, led by their leader Lamoriello and his wisely-chosen coach, Schoenfeld, toasted the players in Chicago Stadium's cramped but jubilant visitors' locker room.

"It still hasn't quite sunk in," chortled Joe Cirella, architect of MacLean's classic.

Oh, it took time, to be sure, but the facts were there for all who took the time to check. With the unlikely victory, the Devils finished with 82 points, 18 more than their previous high a year earlier.

They finished with a record of 38–36–6,

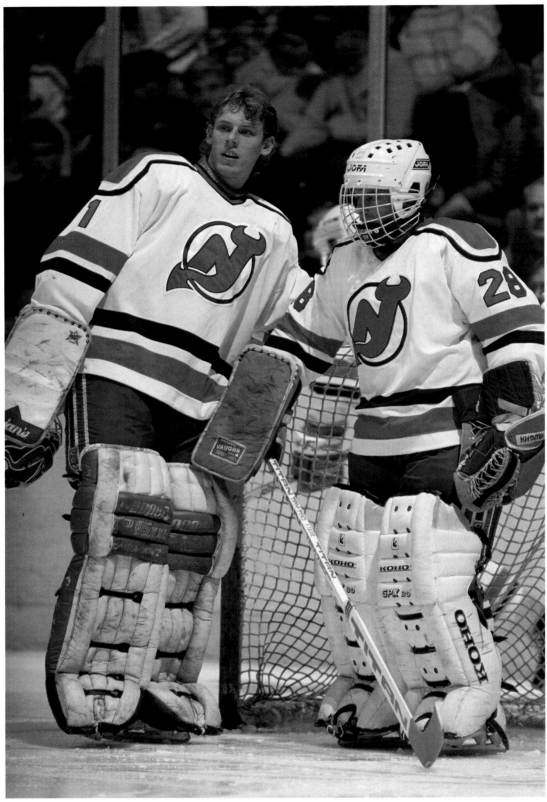

Burke and Sauve—the combination of youth and experience appeared unbeatable.

the first winning season in franchise history. They finished tied with the Rangers in points but won the last Patrick playoff spot with more victories, 38 to the Rangers' 36 under the tiebreaker.

Sean Burke, who kept insisting that he could not be the Devils' savior, posted a 10–1–0 record and 3.05 goals against average. There were many stories of heroism on New Jersey's roster, but none topped the Burke saga.

Under Lamoriello, the club had come of age. The Devils scored the second largest number of goals 295 (3.69 per game) in the team's history (they scored 300 in 1985-86). Defensively, the team set a club record for fewest goals against with 296 (3.70 per game), the first time ever that New Jersey managed to yield fewer than 300 goals against.

Just about everyone in the lineup rated kudos but some of the more special individuals were:

• SEAN BURKE — Following his Olympic stint, Burke did everything but walk on water for the Devils. His mental toughness was remarkable considering he joined a club which literally could not afford to lose more than ONE game; he played his angles confidently and skated fluidly in the crease.

• BOB SAUVE — Lamoriello called Sauve's kick-save on Ken Priestlay's breakaway in the 2–2 tie with Buffalo on March 25 "the biggest save in franchise history." The little guy came through when it counted.

• JOHN MacLEAN — After floundering under the Doug Carpenter administration, Johnny Mac found himself once Schoenfeld took command. The Devils would not have reached the playoffs were it not for his dramatic pair of goals against Chicago. His name became forever etched in Devils history after his heroics in Chicago Stadium.

• KIRK MULLER — The young captain had character, work ethic, and a strong physical presence. Add that to his team leading 37–57–94, all career bests. He had 19 power play goals and 215 shots on goal while providing a clutch effort all year.

• PAT VERBEEK — He led the team in goals (46), game-winning goals (8), and plus-minus (plus-29) while setting personal highs in points (77), goals, and assists (31). Verbeek's penalty shot against the Rangers' Vanbiesbrouck in the final meeting between the clubs did more psychological damage to New York than anything.

• AARON BROTEN — Played in 519 career regular season contests and set career highs for points (83) and assists (57) and shared club lead in assists. He scored a penalty shot on March 24, 1988, against the Blues in the big playoff drive.

• CLAUDE LOISELLE — The defensive specialist finished with a career-high 17 goals including that huge shorthanded score against Washington on March 20, not to mention his sixth goal in ten games on April 2 against the Islanders.

• DOUG BROWN — Like Loiselle, he was an extraordinary penalty killer who led all rookies in shorthanded goals. He, too, got a BIG one in that great, great turnaround game against Washington on March 20.

• JOE CIRELLA — He played the best hockey of his life in the final month of the season and finished with a team-high plus-minus for defensemen (plus-15). Cirella's clutch play at the left point in Game 80 led to MacLean's playoff-clinching goal.

• BRUCE DRIVER — With career highs in goals (15), assists (40), and points (55), Driver established himself as New Jersey's primary offensive threat from the blueline and was the club's leading defenseman in goals, assists, power play scores (7), and shots (190).

So, IT had happened. The Devils were finally competing for the Stanley Cup. In the end it could be said that Lamoriello's decision to replace Carpenter with Schoenfeld was the right move.

"Once we got to the playoffs," said Craig Wolanin, "Jim said, 'Let's beat the Islanders. We can beat the Islanders.' He made us believe in ourselves."

Few others believed in New Jersey. In the minds of most experts, the Devils had gone as far as they could go in reaching the promised land of fourth place. They would now take on the prideful Patrick Division-winning New York Islanders in the opening round.

"Hey," said fast-improving defenseman Ken Daneyko, "if we beat out the Rangers anything is possible. Let's see what happens."

What happened, as they say, is history. With a capital H.

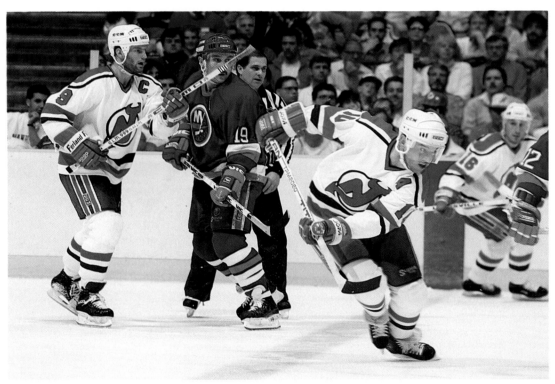

Muller, Broten and Verbeek formed the Devils' top line and were at the heart of the team's attack.

9

BRING ON THE ISLANDERS

According to the pre-playoff analysts, the Devils would be quite fortunate to exit their first-ever Stanley Cup round with one victory. This was not so much an attempt to denigrate the skates from West of the Hudson as much as it was a tribute to the Islanders.

New Jersey was facing a club that still was savoring its four straight Stanley Cup run from 1980 through 1983 and could summon enough power to finish on top of the Patrick Division.

Many of the Islanders Cup heroes, such as captain Denis Potvin and Ken Morrow, still graced their lineup. They had experience, pride and whatever other intangibles go into the fabric of champions. There was only one problem; they didn't bargain for Devils spirit.

The Islanders learned about it at 28 minutes and 31 seconds into Game One at Nassau Coliseum. Craig Wolanin had cut the Isles lead to 2–1 when it became appar-

ent that New Jersey was playing a brand of in-your-face hockey to which the home club was not accustomed.

And when the Isles went up 3–1, again the Devils came back and made it 3–2 and then 3–3. "They never give up," said the Isles leader Pat LaFontaine. "They keep grinding."

It was a bruising game, and it was the Islanders who absorbed most of the bruises. On it went into overtime and at 6:11 LaFontaine beat Sean Burke and the game was over. The home team had won, yet there was a feeling of utter sobriety in the winner's dressing room; almost as if they had met a foe that worried them.

"They're a team with a lot of character-type players," said the Islanders' president and general manager Bill Torrey. "They really work. They have good goaltending and sound defense. They're disciplined and determined."

The Devils hit so many Islanders so

Sean Burke smothered everything that came his way.

often, it inspired some of the New York players to suggest a rivalry had heated to the white-hot stage in a matter of three periods-plus.

"This could get heated," said Torrey. "Give the Devils credit; they didn't give up without a fight."

Meanwhile, the losers sounded like winners. "Our guys were ready to play," said Schoenfeld, "and if they play the whole series like that, it's going to be a good series and a long one."

Schoenfeld could afford to be optimistic. Just when his team appeared to be beaten, John MacLean, whose goals tied and won the overtime game against Chicago, deflected a Bruce Driver shot past Kelly Hrudey with 1:56 to play in regulation.

"We were a little tentative at first because we had never been in the playoffs," said MacLean. "Now we know what it takes."

Game Two was played at Nassau Coliseum the following night. Like just about everyone in the packed arena, the Islanders had expected Schoenfeld to start his young ace Sean Burke in Game Two. Instead, little Bob Sauve was in the net.

In the press box, members of the media insisted that it was a move of desperation and would likely backfire on the Devils. On the ice, it was an entirely different story. A seasoned, unflappable veteran, Sauve played his angles to perfection and left the ice with a 3–2 victory, giving the Devils a much-desired even split on foreign ice.

MacLean, Claude Loiselle, and Mark Johnson were the scorers, with Johnson scoring the winner. Now the series shifted to New Jersey, and, of course, the conjecture centered around Schoenfeld's choice of goaltender. Would he stick with the winner, Sauve, or go back to his money-man, Burke?

Schoenfeld started Big Sean, and if ever a choice was perspicacious, this was it.

Before a roaring sellout crowd of 19,040 at Meadowlands Arena, Burke blanked the Islanders 3–0, giving the Devils their first edge in the series, two games to one.

The 21-year-old goaltender stopped 31 shots in earning the victory. Oddly enough, the game-winner was scored by defenseman Ken Daneyko who bounced a shot off Islander defenseman Tomas Jonsson's stick. Mark Johnson followed with two more tallies while Burke took care of the rest of business.

Amazingly, the Devils had an opportunity to take a 3–1 series lead with the next game on home ice. To say the Islanders were reeling would be an understatement. New Jersey skaters were relentless in their

Schoenfeld had the whole team believing by now.

The Isles were learning the hard way.

checking and the goaltending—be it Burke or Sauve—was close to flawless.

If nothing else, the Devils learned in Game Four that it is foolish to count out champions until they are officially out. This elementary lesson of professional sports was delivered before an incredulous crowd at Byrne Arena on April 10, 1988.

The Devils jumped to a 3–0 lead at 16:50 of the second period and Terry Simpson, the Islanders coach, seemed very close to pulling Hrudey. But he chose not to, and Alan Kerr reduced the lead to 3–1 just 71 seconds before the end of the period.

Although the Devils tightened up, Brent Sutter scored at 11:30 of the third to make it

only 3–2 for New Jersey, and before you knew it the game was tied 4–4 going into another overtime.

What made the Devils defeat so difficult to swallow was the overtime, in which the Islanders were shorthanded three times but won it on Brent Sutter's shorthanded score, only the second in Stanley Cup history.

"When you have the lead and don't have enough to hang on," lamented Schoenfeld, "it's disheartening. But by the time the puck is dropped for the next game, I'm sure our guys will be flying high, believing in themselves. That's just the way this team is."

Nobody could be quite sure whether the

coach was transmitting propaganda or actually believed his words. After all, the Devils had never been in a playoff before, so it was difficult to be certain. "As far as we're concerned," he went on, "this series is even, just like it was a week ago."

It was even and it was evident that the Islanders really had to struggle for their two wins; much more so than New Jersey did for its pair. Whatever the case, the series shifted back to Nassau for Game Five, and few, if any, knew what to make of the rivalry.

If nothing else, the Devils said they would learn from the harrowing, come-from-behind defeat and they were true to their word. They were hardly fazed by the return to hostile ice. Hard-working utility player Pat Conacher said Game Four was the club's alarm clock. In Game Five he underlined his point at 13:12 of the second period with New Jersey ahead 2–1.

Mark Johnson was in the penalty box when Conacher went into orbit on a two-on-one with Aaron Broten. Denis Potvin tried to read the play, expecting a pass but Conacher never thought about passing. He moved to the left face-off circle and whacked a slapshot past Hrudey's right skate and into the far side.

"I was just trying to put it on net," said Conacher. "I was a little intimidated by Potvin, who's a big guy, being there. I just wanted to shoot and go to the net because there were two of us."

The Islanders returned with a quick goal by Tomas Jonsson, but Broten came through with a 45-footer that fooled Hrudey and the Devils annexed the game, 4–2.

To a man, the Devils insisted that they had learned from their overtime blunder and they would not make that kind of mistake again. "In the past," said Verbeek, "we made a huge load of mistakes, but Jim Schoenfeld is big on constant repetition and tells us, 'Don't make the same mistake.' It eventually sinks in."

As for the sinking, that would have to be the state of the Islanders. Down three games to two, they returned to The Meadowlands for Game Six. New York's bravado was gone. The hit men of New Jersey, especially Perry Anderson, Claude Loiselle, and Ken Daneyko were punishing the smaller Islanders relentlessly and with a minimum of return fire. A stern message had been delivered.

"We underestimated them to a certain extent," said Islanders assistant coach Bob Nystrom. "We got the feeling that they would quit, but, obviously, they don't go that route."

Nor could anyone accuse the Islanders of quitting. Trailing 6–1 in the third period at Byrne, Terry Simpson's stickhandlers staged one of the more remarkable of modern playoff rallies, pulling to within one goal in the dying seconds of the match. And even then, the irrepressible LaFontaine broke through the Devils' defense and launched a final shot which Burke managed to save.

"It was so typical of this team," said Joe Cirella. "We've always had to do everything the hard way. Nothing is ever easy for us. We weren't very pretty at the end, but we won."

That was the bottom line; the Devils had won. It was not a fluke win but one that was accomplished at all critical areas of the ice, starting in goal and ending with timely scoring. It was a victory that merely confirmed the veracity of the late-season flourish of wins, and it was a conquest that, once and for all, put the Devils in the Top Banana position among the Metropolitan Area's bunch of hockey teams.

Newsday columnist Joe Gergen put it as well as anyone when he noted: "After five

Second only to Broten in seniority, Joe Cirella savored the on-ice handshakes . . .

. . . before commencing to the dressing room glad-handing with Dr. McMullen.

seasons of residing in the anonymity of a Jersey swamp, so near to and yet so far from the bright lights of the big city, members of the National Hockey League's formerly forgotten franchise have emerged as principal characters in a New York hockey drama."

Like other believers, Gergen lauded the Devils' "talent, tenacity and exquisite timing," and pointed out that the win over the Islanders gave them "a more noble achievement — winning the Patrick Division semi-finals."

To a man, the Devils were justifiably bursting with pride. "It's not the new team on the block anymore," said Mark Johnson. "It's the New Jersey Devils now."

Aaron Broten: "A lot of people are taking notice. All the media attention is on us. We're in a situation where we didn't have time to think about being in the playoffs. We didn't get in until the last night and then we only had a day and a half to get ready. There was no time to dwell on it. Now that we took care of the Islanders, we'll dwell on it a little."

McMullen and John Whitehead shared smiles with Pat Conacher and Dave Maley, who had teamed with Claude Loiselle and Doug Brown to stifle New York's offense.

The truth was, Broten and friends had preciously little moments for any kind of musing over their latest mini-miracle. After all, there was more hockey to be played. Washington's Capitals had disposed of the Philadelphia Flyers and were eagerly await-ing a shot at the upstarts from The Meadowlands.

If there was a Devils bubble to burst, the Caps figured they had the howitzers to explode any more offensives out of Byrne Arena.

By now the confidence was flowing.

10

CAPITAL PUNISHMENT

Granted, Washington was a distinct favorite to beat the Devils, but there were elements of enthusiasm in the New Jersey camp that simply could not be overlooked.

Over the season the Devils had developed a truly solid front line comprised of captain Kirk Muller, vigorous Pat Verbeek, and deceptive Aaron Broten. Patrik Sundstrom, who struggled earlier in the year, was showing signs of rebounding, and generally overlooked youngsters such as Dave Maley and Tom Kurvers were beginning to make an imprint. And, of course, there was Sean Burke's Grade-A goaltending and the reassurance that, at any given time, Bob Sauve could be summoned to the crease and deliver a first-rate effort.

Nobody could quibble with the coaching either. Jim Schoenfeld had devised the best possible battle plan for beating the Islanders and adroitly used reserves such as Pat Conacher, Claude Loiselle, and Doug Brown while getting superior hockey out of

veteran Mark Johnson.

"Jim stressed aggressive penalty-killing with quick shift changes," Brown said. The penalty-killers were especially effective against the Islanders.

Finally, there was that omnipresent element in winners called confidence. It began building for the Devils down the homestretch, was reinforced with the big win over the Rangers a week before season's end, continued growing after the eleventh-hour triumph at Chicago, and reached a peak when the Islanders were defeated.

"Our confidence began flowing," Verbeek explained. "It's a tough thing, that word 'confidence,' how you get it. But this team has gotten it, and we believe in ourselves."

Ah, but so did the Washington Capitals, and that is why the Patrick Division finals was such a dandy. Here were two determined teams hellbent on reaching the Wales Conference championship and

For Broten the playoff run was a dream come true.

unwilling to concede an inch of ice in the process.

Among the Devils who most epitomized this spirit was fireplug forward Conacher. "I got called up from Utica the same day they fired Doug Carpenter," Conacher was saying before the start of the Washington series. "I don't know if the team was struggling or if they wanted to shake things up a little."

Of course they had been struggling and, to no one's surprise, Patty did shake up the Devils. He was a pro's pro; a 29-year-old who, at 5–8, 180 pounds, was deemed unworthy of the NHL by the Rangers and, to a certain extent, Doug Carpenter. Conacher rolled with the punches until he was elevated by Lamoriello and given a role by Schoenfeld. He became left wing on the Devils' checking line with Loiselle and

Brown, not to mention a key element in the penalty-killing force.

No less important was defenseman Joe Cirella, a low-key backliner who had occasionally been jeered by New Jersey fans for what they perceived as indifferent play. Cirella, who had played for the Colorado Rockies, had reached his peak in the latter part of the season and the playoffs.

"It was quite a thrill to finally be able to know what it feels like to be IN the playoffs," said Cirella.

Teammate Broten also was an alumnus of the Rockies. "It didn't bother me that much that we were down in the early years of the franchise," said Broten, "because we always thought we were improving. We'd always say, 'Next year we'll make the playoffs.' But even with 16 teams it was hard to get in there."

In the Capitals, the Devils would meet a team that had frequently disappointed in playoffs past. This time, however, they were coming off an inspirational seven-game win over the Flyers. "They're similar to our team," said Burke, "in that they rely on everybody to chip in. You can't key on one guy, or another guy will burn you."

Finally, for the Devils' high command there was the foreign-ice factor. Would the Monster of the Cap Centre destroy them? The Devils had an awful 0–19–1 streak at the Landover, Maryland, rink until they rallied for their epic 4–2 triumph on March 20.

"It won't bother us," said MacLean. "We had a 1–19–1 record at the Nassau Coliseum before we opened our playoff with the Islanders, and we beat them two out of three there."

Never mind who would win; how long would the series go?

Washington Coach Bryan Murray opined that it would be a long one. "It appears it'll be a six- or seven-game series the way we played against the Flyers and they played against the Islanders," Murray said. "We're similar in lots of ways. We're two teams that work hard and are very entertaining."

Could the Devils do it again?

"Yes, we can do it again," defenseman Randy Velischek insisted. "The way we're playing now, we can beat any team we have to play."

But not the way they played in Game One. At seven minutes and 18 seconds of the first period Mike Ridley beat Burke, and from that point on Washington gained control of the tempo. Early in the second period Larry Murphy popped a high one past Burke from the slot on a Caps power play, and later in the period Burke misjudged Scott Stevens' shot. Tom Kurvers spoiled Pete Peeter's shutout in the third period but, by then, it didn't matter. The final score was 3–1 for Washington in a game about which the New York *Times* noted, "The Devils' intensity fell."

Kurvers put it another way. "We weren't finishing well."

Well, at least one Devil did, and because of that, controversy flared like an out-of-control forest fire. Late in the third period Verbeek attempted to check an onrushing Rod Langway along the left boards. Langway went down with a severe cut on the back of his left leg and had to be escorted from the arena on crutches.

The often vitriolic Murray charged that Verbeek had deliberately attempted to injure his player, a charge that was quickly squelched by the Devil. "I just stuck my leg out to make sure Langway didn't get away from me," Verbeek explained. "I wasn't trying to injure him. I'm not that kind of player."

Meanwhile, the Capitals' Mike Gartner was busily denying that he tried to hurt Sundstrom, whose leg also was wounded in a collision. "He came at me," said Gartner,

"and I planted my leg to check him. He hit my leg, ran into it. I didn't stick my leg out and try to injure him."

If the Devils were down, they didn't betray any lack of confidence about Game Two, also at Landover. Burke summed up prevailing opinion when he asserted, "We lost the first game to the Islanders and came back to win the second one."

Amen. But at Nassau, Schoenfeld pulled his change-up and sent Sauve into the net. This time it would be Burke in Game Two.

Plain and simply, war broke out before the second playoff game had ended. Inflamed by headlines suggesting that it would be a "grudge match" to atone for Langway's injury—he would be out for the entire series—the Capitals tried to get physical with New Jersey and learned the same lesson that the Islanders did: it was a mistake.

The Devils won most of the battles and the war as well. For coach Schoenfeld, the most important development was the increased desire displayed by his troops. They got the jump on Washington with Broten's power play goal at 9:37 of the first period and, although Ridley tied the count shortly thereafter, never fell behind.

With the score tied 1–1 early in the second period Broten added two more goals for a hat trick. Larry Murphy got one back for the home team late in the period, but Verbeek answered that one at 18:14 giving the Devils a two-goal cushion entering the third frame. Sundstrom closed the scoring with another power play score at 12:49 of the finale.

As for the hand-to-hand combat, it began at 3:31 of the second period when a brawl totalling 70 penalty minutes took place. Heavyweight Ed Kastelic of Washington threw Loiselle to the ice, and the two started fighting. Perry Anderson and Greg Smith squared off next, followed by Yvon

Corriveau and Kurvers. Then Kastelic skated over to Anderson, who was on top of Smith, and began punching him from behind.

Schoenfeld was pleased that his club was not intimidated. "Our team has really good hockey courage," he said. "A game like this lets us show it. It doesn't matter if we lost a scrap because we came right back. A lot of guys got their noses dirty and their intensity level up."

Verbeek, who was a special target of the 18,130 spectators, never flinched in combat and gave it right back in the best manner possible, a key goal. "Our team likes rough games," said Patty. "They seem to get us more involved and more excited. And we don't get intimidated."

It was, however, only a game. The series was tied at one apiece and would resume in New Jersey. Meanwhile, the war of the words continued. Still incensed over the Langway injury, the Capitals sent tapes of the collision to NHL executive vice-president Brian O'Neill in an attempt to inspire the league to suspend the Devil. O'Neill summarily rejected the attempt made by Washington general manager David Poile.

"I reviewed the tape of the incident," said O'Neill. "In my judgment, it requires no further action by the league. It was just an unfortunate accident."

In some quarters it was hinted that the Caps were panicking. The contrast between the excitable Murray and the laconic Schoenfeld was striking; not that Jersey's Redhead II wasn't given to the occasional roar. But Schoenfeld had by now a firm grip on his team, and it showed.

"The story of this year is the hiring of Schoenfeld," said Devils executive vice president Max McNab. "Lou made a dramatic move and Jim turned that last corner for this franchise. It is amazing how timing is so important in life. I thought Doug

Carpenter did a good job while he was here, but I don't believe the result would have been the same without Schoenfeld. He was so clearly the right kind of person at the right time."

Would the Devils be the "right kind" of players in their first home game of the Patrick Division finals on home ice. Newark *Star-Ledger* columnist Walter MacPeek offered this suggestion:

"The Devils must harness their emotions and block out the distractions. They must do what they do best: Outwork opponents."

And did they ever!

Would you believe, 10–4.

Sundstrom savored an unprecedented eight-point performance in one of the most memorable scoring feasts at Byrne Arena.

How great was it? Consider this: Mark Johnson scored four goals — two in the first and two in the third periods — and was virtually overlooked in the afterglow of victory.

This was inevitable considering that Sundstrom had a hat trick AND five assists, breaking the playoff record of seven points, set three times by Wayne Gretzky.

"Eight points," laughed Johnson. "That's a touchdown and a two-point conversion. Gretzky has scored a ton of points, but he never had a night like this."

Special teams were decisive in the first period. The Devils made good on two of three power plays while the Caps succeeded on one of two and New Jersey took a 2–1 lead to the dressing room after the first 20 minutes.

In the second period the Devils capitalized on Washington mistakes in their defensive zone and scored twice in two minutes, beginning with Sundstrom's first at 57 seconds and followed by Loiselle's shorthanded score at 2:01. Washington stayed close with a pair of goals to trim the margin to 4–3. Then the Devils answered with three to the Capitals' one, and the

A media avalanche covered Sundstrom (eight points) and Johnson (four goals) after the 10–4 rout of Washington.

second period ended with Schoenfeld's sextet ahead 7–4.

Johnson's third and fourth, followed by Sundstrom's third, wrapped up the rout in the third, which featured a continuation of the conflict that had erupted in Game Two. "At one point," said Maley, "Kevin Hatcher hit me in the jaw with his stick. I went down and I was out. It was a cheap shot. It was a dirty game."

Frank Brown of the *Daily News* took in the rough stuff and had this commentary: "The Capitals are still trying to impale Verbeek for accidentally cutting Langway's left leg. They're still trying to tell the Devils they won't be pushed around. The Devils aren't listening."

Nor were the Capitals dead. They had rallied from a three game to one deficit against the Flyers and believed they could rally against the Devils.

And they did. Not only that, they won Game Four, 4–1, despite a blast by MacLean that knocked Washington goalie Pete Peeters unconscious. Peeters was taken off the ice on a stretcher in full uniform and remained overnight at Hackensack Hospital for observation. Coincidentally, Caps defenseman Garry Galley was struck in the left temple when he blocked a shot by Broten in the third period and also was hospitalized with a possible concussion.

Peeters was replaced by Clint Malarchuk who stopped 13 shots and protected the 3–1 lead after the Devils had gone ahead 1–0 on Kurvers' first period power-play goal. Once Dave Christian tied the score and Peter Sundstrom put the visitors ahead, it was all Washington. So, it was back to Maryland for Game Five in a series that had now become a toss-up.

"It seems that when we play our best is when we have our biggest challenge," said Mark Johnson, one of the Devils' scorers and a member of the miracle 1980 U.S. Olympic team. "We've still got a way to go before being compared to that Gold Medal club, but they were underdogs and we are, too."

In a sense the Capitals were underdogs of a sort. Their reputation for blowing playoffs was so legendary that even G.M. David Poile could kid about it. "One paper wrote, 'If the Capitals were Indians, Custer would still be alive,'" Poile recalled. "I had to admit, it was a great line."

Almost as great as the one Schoenfeld pulled when he announced before Game Five, "Bob Sauve is replacing Sean Burke tonight."

Simple, but eloquent. The declaration spoke volumes about the coach's confidence in himself and his second goalie. But no matter how you shake it, The Redhead was taking a momumental gamble.

Starting his 31st Stanley Cup game, Sauve was typically calm, and his teammates responded in kind. They built up a two-goal lead on goals by Muller and Kurvers and then tightened the defensive vise. Washington didn't score until there was 9:36 remaining. That made it a scary 2–1 with enough time for Washington to score again, but then captain Kirk delivered his second goal and that finally cemented the victory. The 3–1 decision had put New Jersey just one win away from The Final Four.

Schoenfeld, deservedly, was glowing over his goaltending switch. After all, he pointed out, Burke had played in nine of the Devils' eleven playoff games.

"Sean responds to a heavy work load," said the coach. "Bob has supported us with the ability not to use him and then count on him when we do. I have complete confidence anytime I call on Bobby. He's just remarkable. There aren't that many goalies that can play as infrequently and come in and stand on his ear like he does."

Coaches, as a rule, do not favor breaking up winning combinations. Logic dictated that Schoenfeld would come back with Sauve in Game Six, but Redhead II decided to play it close to the vest until game time, when Burke got the nod.

It was one of the few coaching mistakes Schoenfeld had made, but it was a whopper. Washington scored five goals against Burke in two periods, sending him to the shower. Sauve took over for the final period and permitted two more scores. The Capitals had overwhelmed New Jersey, 7–2.

If ever a coach was on the spot, Schoenfeld was that man as the decisive Game Seven approached. Would it be Sauve who suddenly seemed more dependable, or would it be Burke, who was so easily solved in Game Six by the Capitals?

The decision was made in unusual circumstances. After Friday's day-of-game skate, Schoenfeld walked into the locker room and found Burke taking a shower.

"Schony threw me the soap," Burke recalled, "and I dropped it. Then, he threw it at me again—and I dropped it. But I caught it on the third try, and he said I was playing."

Schoenfeld was asked about his decision, particularly in view of the fact that Burke dropped the first two soap-tosses. "Yeah, he dropped the first two," said the coach, "but he kept the soap in front of him. And I figured we would win if he only gave up two, anyway."

The words were cute, but the gamble was still immense. Much would depend on how Burke reacted to this critical decision in his favor. "I'm thankful as anything that Coach Schoenfeld showed that confidence in me because I did have a lousy game in Game Six and I wasn't happy with the way I played. And any time you have a game like that, you want to go right back as quickly as you can and get back in there. It would

have been understandable if he had gone with Bob because he has been playing great hockey for us."

And so with 18,130 Capital Centre fans roaring for the home club, the pad-encumbered Burke walked out of the visiting team's dressing room door and led his teammates on to the hostile ice. If the roaring crowd had any negative effect on the Devils, it was not apparent from their performance from the opening face-off. They instantly challenged the Capitals and scored within 18 seconds when Muller took a pass from Broten and beat Peeters from the low slot with a wristshot. Four shots later Loiselle redirected a Driver slapshot past Peeters for a 2–0 lead at 12:01 of the period.

While all this was going on, New Jersey penalty killers put on a peerless performance. They killed five disadvantages through the 15-minute mark of the second period. The Devils figured that if they could exit the second frame up by two, then they could stifle Washington in the third period.

Whether it was a letdown, a bad break or whatever, this luxury would not be available. Five seconds after a Washington power play had expired, Grant Ledyard fired a slapshot from the left side that beat Burke at 15:21, and before they could escape with a one-goal lead, the Devils permitted Garry Galley to tie the count with six seconds remaining in the period.

The cacophony that greeted the Capitals as they strode to the ice for period three signalled the kind of inspiration that would have demoralized a team with less fibre than New Jersey. Many veteran hockey observers—including John Cunniff, then representing the Bruins who awaited the winner—expected the Devils to cave in as the third period unfolded.

"I'm surprised the Devils had so much poise," said Cunniff. "After the Capitals

The Devils had an answer . . .

scored that fluke goal by Galley, they could have just fallen apart. But New Jersey was very poised in the third, and Burke came up with a couple of great saves. That was a case of remarkable confidence under pressure.''

And did the pressure ever mount. After five minutes the score was 2–2. It remained 2–2 after ten minutes; then eleven, then twelve and thirteen. "It was fascinating,'' added Cunniff. "The Devils were such a young team and in the playoffs for the first time — and in a seventh game for the first time; and getting late into the third period of the seventh game against a much more experienced team, yet they were keeping their cool and THAT was impressive.''

As the seconds ticked off into the thirteenth minute of the third period, an aura of sudden-death enveloped the arena. There

. . . for everything . . .

was the general feeling that the next goal—no matter which team scored it—would be the winner.

Washington had the better of the play so far in the period, but Burke was as splendid as Schoenfeld had hoped he would be when he made the goaltending choice. On one of the Devils' forays into the enemy zone, the puck was skimmed by Mark Johnson to Craig Wolanin at the right point. "Wooly,"

as he was known to his mates, had a mighty shot but never seemed to use it enough to suit his detractors. On this occasion, he wasted little time.

The drive was vicious and on net, but before it ever reached its destination, John MacLean—camped in front of the crease—extended his stick and tipped the puck past goalie Peeters for his fifth goal of the play-offs. Silence enveloped the Cap Centre. The

. . . Washington had to offer.

time was 13:39, and now it was Burke's game to preserve.

"I had something to prove to myself and to everybody that I could fight back from a game like Game Six and be a plus for my team," Burke said later.

"The Capitals did a lot of things to distract Sean," said Schoenfeld, "but he kept his composure despite the distractions."

Slowly and almost painfully, the minutes were consumed as the third period came to a finish. Time and time again, the desperate Capitals attempted to dissect the New Jersey defense for one last assault at Burke, but they were thwarted; and when the shots did get through, Sean defused them with aplomb.

"He really came through for us in the third period," Schoenfeld asserted.

The final score was 3–2. A human wall of bodies wearing red, green, and white descended on Burke in the typical congratulatory ritual. Once every Devil had hugged a teammate, the players lined up for the traditional handshake with the enemy and then on to the dressing room for the post-triumph celebration.

The overflowing Devils dressing room resembled the classic skateroom scene from the Marx Brothers film "A Night At The Opera." Visiting newsmen had to step over bodies while television cameramen jockeyed for position.

Owner John McMullen, easily one of the happiest in the room, personally congratulated his players, as did Lamoriello, who presented Schoenfeld with a "New Jersey Devils: 1988 Patrick Division Playoff Champions" T-shirt.

"I feel privileged to be the coach of this team," Schoenfeld said. "I feel so proud of these guys. I just haven't seen a group like this."

Kudos for the team built by Lamoriello came from everywhere, even Edmonton, where broadcaster and Edmonton *Journal* columnist John Short toasted the new Patrick Division champions. "Only one clear conclusion is possible after the Devils shocked Washington," said Short. "The Devils are in the Prince of Wales final because they were the best team when it counted. No other reason need to be considered. In the deciding game, the Devils proved themselves to be better in goal, deeper on defense, better behind the bench, more emotional, stronger physically, generally faster, and capable of winning all the important faceoffs. Besides, they were luckier. Good teams usually are."

And like all good teams, the Devils developed a legitimate hero. Like Tommy Henrich, "Old Reliable" of championship New York Yankees teams past, John MacLean had emerged as the clutch scorer supreme, again delivering the winning counter when it was most needed.

"I want to continue this dream," exculted MacLean in the jubilant dressing room. "Please don't wake me up."

Sorry, John, but the scheduling demands of the National Hockey League couldn't accommodate you. Soon after the last handshake was exchanged, the Devils had to pack up and take a jet to Beantown. The Wales Conference finals, starting at Boston Garden, was just hours away.

Tom Kurvers added life to the power play all year.

11

TAKING ON
THE BRUINS

By the time the Devils' plane had landed at Boston's Logan International Airport, the doughty denizens of Byrne Arena had captured the imagination of sports fans across the country. If they hadn't come from New Jersey, you would have thought the team's name was Cinderella Devils.

Pulitzer Prize-winning New York *Times* columnist Dave Anderson rhapsodized over John McMullen's team in a manner that was unusual for this usually staid author.

"Until now," wrote Anderson, "Byrne Meadowlands Arena was just a structure. But because of the New Jersey Devils, it's now a structure with soul. Because of the Devils, it finally has some memories. And as a result, some meaning. Jersey fans will cherish Sean Burke's frantic final-second save in the sixth game elimination of the Islanders. In the series with the Caps there is the memory of Patrik Sundstrom's record eight points and Mark Johnson's four goals.

"At the toll booths people can now point to the arena and say that's where Patrik Sundstrom produced more points in a Stanley Cup game than Wayne Gretzky, Gordie Howe or Maurice (Rocket) Richard ever did in any other rink."

And for the first time a banner hung from the rafters: "1988 PATRICK DIVISION PLAYOFF CHAMPIONS."

Toronto *Sun* columnist Jim Hunt took due note of it and said, "My vote goes to the Devils as the Cinderella story of the year. The way they play no team is safe, even Wayne Gretzky and the Oilers. The Devils used to be a bigger joke than the Leafs. They've risen from the ashes and are for real."

Waiting at Boston Garden, Bruins coach Terry O'Reilly wondered just how real his next opponents really were and just how to prepare for them. Nobody was quite certain, despite intensive scouting. If anything, Schoenfeld had thoroughly confused the opposition.

Lamoriello's mid-season choice was looking better by the week, and now he was ready to toss another curve. He would open the series for the first time with Sauve in goal rather than Burke. After what Schoenfeld had done so far, who could quibble?

But as had happened against both the Islanders and Capitals, inertia had set in along the Devils bench. They were back on their haunches and found themselves trailing 0–3 while the Bruins roamed free over Boston Garden ice.

"It took us a while until we realized that we could play with them," explained Tom Kurvers.

That accomplished, the visitors turned on all cylinders. Kurvers tipped Aaron Broten's centering pass inside the right post at 11:26 of the second period for the Devils' first goal, and a point shot by Jack O'Callahan deflected off Craig Janney's skate to bring them within a goal at 13:45. They pulled even at 2:48 of the third period on a power-play screen shot by Kurvers from just above the left circle.

The comeback was vintage Devils, but they could hold the tie for less than four minutes. Keith Crowder's shot just short of the six-minute mark rebounded to Ray Bourque. The Norris Trophy-winner pounced on the loose puck and fired it past Sauve. The time was 5:56. Ken Linseman added an insurance goal with 3:55 to go to settle the issue.

"The Bruins," confessed Schoenfeld, "are not a team you can spot three goals. They were ready to play hockey."

Naturally, Schoenfeld was second-guessed all over town for starting Sauve. He explained, "I wanted to let EVERYONE come down after the win over Washington. I didn't let either goalie know until they had a good night's sleep, and just let them prepare for the game. And I feel I can win with Bob."

Nevertheless, Burke was between the pipes to start Game Two, also at Boston. Bruins players argued that they would be even better prepared than they had been in the opener and would never, ever, allow another blown three-goal lead. The Devils came away from the loss persuaded—as they had been on Long Island and in Maryland—that they were worthy competitors.

For the third straight series, they went about delivering the message on the ice. After Keith Crowder had given the Bruins a 1–0 power-play lead at 4:38, the Devils came back with goals by Pat Verbeek and Aaron Broten within six minutes of the first period and held their lead through the second period.

Burke was outstanding well into the third period as the Devils' checkers thoroughly frustrated Boston. With 4:09 remaining in regulation time, referee Kerry Fraser hit Doug Sulliman with a questionable hooking penalty after he came together with Bruins defenseman Michael Thelven. Toronto *Sun* writer Scott Morrison said, "It was a dive," but the penalty held up anyway.

With the power play in motion, Bob Joyce of the Bruins maneuvered into position for a point blank shot. Burke made a spectacular save but the rebound went right back to Joyce who swiped the bouncing puck toward the net. The puck struck Aaron Broten and spun into the twine.

"I felt," said Schoenfeld, "that with all the things Fraser had let go, he shouldn't have called that one on Sully—and I told him so."

The third period ended tied at two, and the overtime period was as close as the regulation time. Burke robbed Cam Neely of the winning overtime goal on a breakaway, and he also made outstanding saves against Rick Middleton, Craig Janney, and

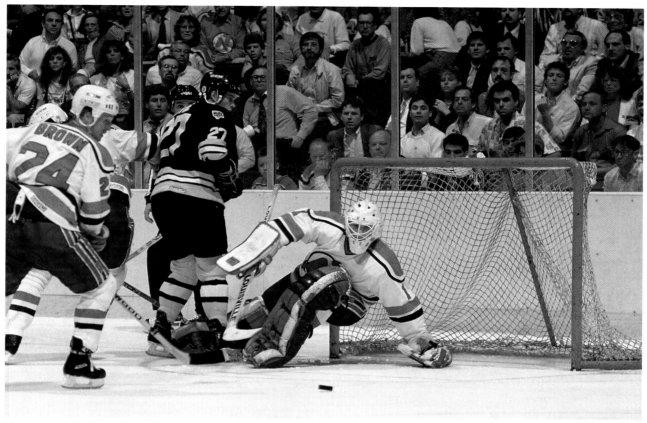

Knowing Burke was behind them lifted the pressure from the Devils' skaters.

Randy Burridge.

Conceivably, the game could stretch to a second sudden-death. Time was fast running out in the first overtime when the Bruins were called for icing the puck, giving the Devils a face-off in the left circle in the Bruins' defensive zone.

Claude Loiselle faced off against Janney, won the draw easily and dispatched the puck to left defenseman Randy Velischek. Instead of shooting, Velischek carried the puck into the left corner behind the net. He moved a pass to Devils right defenseman Joe Cirella. Meanwhile, Doug Brown dropped back into a defensive role to cover for Cirella.

"The guys on the bench were my eyes," Cirella remembered. "I could hear them yelling for me to get the puck to Brownie."

The pass was perfect. Brown released a shot at goalie Reggie Lemelin. A traffic jam helped block Lemelin's view and, said Cirella, "that helped it go in."

The goal light flashed at 17:46 of the period.

"When I saw the puck go in and the red light go on," said Brown, "it was just overwhelming excitement. My body felt electrified. It was the biggest thrill of my life."

Then, a pause from the Southborough native and former Boston College star: "And we couldn't have done it without Sean Burke."

Terry O'Reilly confirmed. "Burke's goaltending was the difference." Since joining the Devils on March 1, 1988, Burke's record had climbed to 17–6 in regular season and playoff games.

In the giddy atmosphere of the winner's dressing room, Schoenfeld's tongue-lashing of referee Fraser was a mere footnote to the gallant performances of Brown, Burke, Verbeek, and Broten. Others talked about how David Maley had made a super save when he stuck his right skate out to block Gord Kluzak's overtime ten-footer from the slot at 3:06 after Burke had stopped Linseman's goalmouth try.

Referee-baiting was nothing new in or out of the playoffs, and neutral observers agreed that Schoenfeld had a legitimate gripe against Fraser. In the minds of most reporters it was gone and forgotten; except for the eruption that followed Game Three at The Meadowlands.

Having tied the series and convinced themselves that they were every bit the Bruins' equal, the Devils looked forward to their homecoming and the opportunity to take a two-to-one lead in the Wales finals.

Whether it was the pregame hullaballoo, overconfidence or whatever, the Devils did not sprint from the blocks the way their coach had anticipated. "I knew after the first three or four shifts of the game that we didn't have the juice. I was hoping we'd score the first goal because I knew if we got into a hole, it would be very, very difficult to get out."

The Devils escaped the first period unscathed. Neither team scored but a double-minor penalty to Verbeek at 19:30 of the first period would leave New Jersey shorthanded into the second. Before they could kill the penalty, Linseman converted a pass from Bourque, putting Boston ahead 1–0.

"We wanted to pick up the tempo after the first period," said Mark Johnson, "and get into the game. But we had to go out and kill those power plays. Then they scored again and we were down 3–0 before we knew it."

Boston led 5–1 at the end of the second period, and Schoenfeld was fit to be tied over referee Don Koharski's officiating. The coach was particularly angry over the referee's handing Verbeek four minutes for roughing while Keith Crowder got only two after a skirmish that appeared to involve both players with equal intensity. Kirk Muller also had two minutes for holding at 19:30 of the first period and it was those series of penalties that led to the Bruins advantage and eventual annexing of the game.

In the third period, for whatever reason, Koharski began calling penalties against Boston long after the winner had, in effect, been decided. This angered some Devils who believed that he was engaged in an official's "evening-up" practice.

The boiling point was reached in the game's final minute when Koharski hit the Devils with a bench penalty for delay of game and then added a holding penalty to Ken Daneyko with 23 seconds remaining.

Boston won the match 6–1, but the events of the previous three periods already had set off a chain reaction of fury that would cause infinite explosions around the league.

12

THE KOHARSKI-NHL UPRISING (YELLOW SUNDAY)

Scores are often deceptive in relation to the actual play on ice. How many times have you heard coaches say, "Sure, we won 4–2, but it would have been 7–4 for them if it weren't for their goaltending."

Sometimes it is goaltending that makes a difference, and on other occasions it is officiating that can tilt a game in a certain direction. Right or wrong, Devils coach Jim Schoenfeld believed that Don Koharski's work as referee in Game Three not only left something to be desired but played a significant role in determining the one-sided score.

Such a reaction is nothing new in hockey. Overwrought coaches — especially after playoff games — have been as common in NHL history as overtime wins. In the 1942 finals between Toronto and Detroit, Red Wings coach Jack Adams was suspended for the remainder of the playoffs after a confrontation with referee Mel Harwood following a Game Four loss to the Maple Leafs. (Adams' team was leading the series, three to one, at the time.) Thus, it was not totally surprising that Schoenfeld was steaming at the conclusion of Game Three, which gave Boston a two games to one series edge.

At the conclusion of the game, Schoenfeld and assistant coach Doug McKay remained at the dasher boards as their players trudged to the dressing room. NHL security director Frank Torpey and at least one other NHL security person remained at the exit with Schoenfeld.

Torpey easily could have ushered Schoenfeld to the Devils' locker area when it became apparent that the coach wanted to talk to the referee, but nothing was done.

Likewise, Koharski, who obviously was aware that the coach was incensed with his performance, easily could have defused the potential explosion merely by remaining at center ice, or a convenient distance, as other referees frequently have done, to allow the coach some cooling time until he eventually left the scene. There was no reason for Koharski to rush toward the officials' room.

Accompanied by linesmen Gord Broseker and Ray Scapinello, Koharski skated to the gate where the coach and referee began their argument. NHL security personnel either did nothing or were ineffective as the dispute quickly escalated in the cramped corridor leading to the dressing rooms.

By this time Meadowlands security personnel moved into the fray, but the melee continued, and, at one point, Koharski lost his balance, slipped off the runway and against a door frame which jutted into the corridor. The referee hit the frame and then the wall but stayed on his feet by catching a corner of the framework with his left hand.

"Oh, you're gone now! You're gone. You won't coach another . . ." shouted Koharski.

Schoenfeld shot back, "You fell and you know it. You know you fell. I didn't touch you."

Koharski: "You're gone. You're gone. And I hope it's on tape."

Schoenfeld: "Good, 'cause you fell you fat pig. Have another doughnut."

Cooler heads finally intervened forcefully and escorted the coach to his left to the Devils' room and the referee to the right to the officials' sanctuary. Koharski continued shouting beligerently down the corridor while Schoenfeld repeated what, in time, would be the deathless line, "Have another doughnut."

The incident had many witnesses including at least one television cameraman who was in position to record some of the collisions. Most of the print media, as is typical in such situations, were either in the press box or waiting in the interview area below, away from the corridor in question.

When Schoenfeld finally met the press, he was blunt about the situation.

"Yes," he acknowledged, "I waited for him after the game. I had some things to say to him about his officiating. I disagreed with a lot of it. He didn't want to hear me. He said I pushed him. He told me, 'You'll never coach again.' He bumped me . . . my hands were at my side."

Koharski would not speak with reporters but did phone NHL executive vice president Brian O'Neill to report on the episode.

Early the next morning the papers were filled with banner headlines. DEVILS COACH IN HOT WATER, blared *Newsday,* echoing the theme throughout the metropolitan area. SCHOENFELD, REFEREE SCUFFLE AFTER BLOWOUT.

If further action would be taken, it would be handled by O'Neill who went to his Montreal office on Saturday morning, the day after the game.

O'Neill told an interviewer that he had not looked at the tape of the incident although Devils president-general manager Lou Lamoriello had offered to send a tape to Montreal. Futhermore, O'Neill never arranged a meeting—customary in such situations—whereby Schoenfeld, Koharski and other participants could discuss the incident.

Throughout Saturday the phone lines were abuzz as various representatives of the aggrieved parties discussed the matter. Among those involved was the lawyer for the NHL Officials Association, Jim Beatty, and Dave Newell, the referee scheduled to handle Game Four at Byrne.

No word came from O'Neill, and no one knew the whereabouts of NHL president John Ziegler, who so far had been incommunicado. Finally, on Mother's Day, May 8, the night on which Game Four was to be played, O'Neill suspended Schoenfeld (for at least one game) for the verbal abuse of Koharski. The question of physical contact, said O'Neill, was still under review.

When, shortly after noon on Mother's Day, O'Neill informed Lamoriello of the decision, the Devils' leader pointed out that no hearing was held and the right of appeal should be honored. The Devils then decided they would attempt to reverse the decision via the courts.

Devils owner Dr. John McMullen approved the plan to take legal action, and the wheels were set in motion for a major confrontation. Obviously, the Jerseyites would not take this with passivity. Lamoriello phoned Gil Stein, the NHL's chief legal counsel, informing him that the club would be seeking a temporary restraining order to overturn Schoenfeld's ban. The case would be considered by Bergen County Superior Court Judge James F. Madden, who agreed to hear the case at his home in Cliffside Park, New Jersey.

Lamoriello, accompanied by the team's general counsel, New York attorney Patrick Gilmartin, and John A. Conte, a Bergen County lawyer, would represent the Devils before the Judge. Among the legal documents presented by Conte included the following:

"The referee, without warning to Plaintiff Coach James Schoenfeld, pushed past him, and through use of threats and intimidation, caused a certain concern and anxiety among those in the area, and stumbled through no fault or cause of Plaintiff Coach James Schoenfeld.

"To avoid charges or misconduct due to his threats and harassment, Referee Donald Koharski deliberately filed a grievance with the National Hockey League, well knowing the sanctions that could be imposed on the Plaintiff Coach James Schoenfeld."

Madden began hearing the case almost simultaneously with the delivery of O'Neill's suspension report to the media at Byrne Arena. It was 6 p.m. and players from both teams were preparing for the game. Referee Dave Newell and his crew also were supposed to be dressing, but the NHL's supervisor of the series, John McCauley, contacted The Meadowlands' off-ice officials and quietly warned that THEY might have to select a referee and two linesmen to handle the game should Newell stage a walkout.

According the Sandy Jenkins, author of *Yellow Sunday,* the definitive book on *l'affaire* Koharski, "Judge Madden said he didn't want to intervene with the operations of a self-regulating body such as the NHL, but the league operates in New Jersey and therefore is subject to New Jersey law."

Jenkins went on to cite the Judge's further interpretation of the events:

"This is the NHL, not some indigent defendent. The NHL, who must have some connections in New York or New Jersey, they suspend the coach of a team in the middle of what is like the World Series and they can't conduct a hearing . . .

"The thing of it is, the NHL's investigation consisted of them calling one person (Koharski), then another (Schoenfeld). In the middle of an important series like this, particularly when they have something like a videotape . . . . What can more conclusive than a photographic production? Plus the fact that after (O'Neill) made up his mind, the Devils asked for a hearing and everyone runs into the woods and gets lost."

Players of both clubs took the ice for their pregame warmup shortly after 7 p.m., yet nobody among the media horde could tell for sure whether the game would begin. Doug McKay was behind the Devils' bench during the skate, but Schoenfeld still was in the dressing room. Nobody — except McCauley and the linesmen — knew whether Newell would officiate.

The game was to begin at 7:45 p.m. Judge Madden made his decision at 7:20 p.m., issuing a temporary, verbal restraining order which stated that Schoenfeld could coach. The Judge phoned McCauley directing the NHL to "desist and refrain from suspending Schoenfeld pending a formal hearing and notice of specific charges against him."

As soon as it possibly could be typed, the Devils issued a prepared statement from Lamoriello to the media:

"The New Jersey Devils cannot tolerate the injustice that has been done to Jim Schoenfeld and our organization. We are owed the right of a hearing and an appeal.

"Two weeks ago, when Brendan Shanahan became involved with a member of the Washington Capitals, the league conducted a hearing in my office within 36 hours of the altercation. Yet in this case, with the future of the franchise at stake as well as the reputation of our coach, Jim Schoenfeld, Brian O'Neill did not convene an official hearing."

The Devils, Lamoriello continued, "regretted having to take such extreme legal measures, but a hearing was required because the officials filed reports to the league which were clearly false. We cannot accept this."

Moreover, independent and objective eyewitnesses had clearly disputed Koharski's claims, and sufficient information had been obtained that the NHL's case was weak. Until this point in time, NHL president John Ziegler was not heard from, nor did anyone admit to a knowledge of his whereabouts.

When Newell and linesmen Gord Broseker and Ray Scapinello learned of the temporary restraining order permitting Schoenfeld to coach, they were advised by their association's lawyer Jim Beatty not to take the ice.

A unique, illegal strike had been called by the NHL officials. The game could not go on without a referee and linesmen.

Aware of this, McCauley asked the New Jersey off-ice officials if they could supply one referee and a pair of linesmen to handle the match. However, players and coaches of both teams had taken the ice and were awaiting the opening face-off when McCauley advised Schoenfeld of the walkout. Eventually, players from both teams returned to the dressing room to await further developments as an aura of excitement and tension enveloped the arena.

The capacity crowd, unaware of the developments in the bowels of the arena, simply awaited the start of play as baseball fans do during a rain delay.

Swinging into action, McCauley attempted to hammer out a deal between Beatty, Lamoriello, and Bruins general manager Harry Sinden. It would have meant an intolerable concession by the Devils and, as Lamoriello later noted, "I was shocked when the officials refused to officiate, but it never occured to me to remove Jim. Two wrongs don't make a right."

Since Ziegler could not be found, McCauley then contacted the highest available NHL executive, William Wirtz, chairman of the league's Board of Governors. Wirtz told the referee and the linesmen that they had a contractual obligation to handle the game, but they still refused to officiate, as did back-up referee Denis Morel.

According to Sandy Jenkins' account, Beatty suggested that Schoenfeld work the game from the press box, via headset. "Sinden rejected Beatty's suggestion by saying, 'We don't need you guys (the NHL game officials)'. In effect, Sinden forced the issue by supporting Lamoriello," Jenkins noted.

Excitement mounted as ways and means of insuring that the game be played were sought. Wirtz had concluded that the show must go on; it only was a question as to the names of the substitute referee and linesmen. Sinden and Lamoriello had agreed

Off-ice official Paul McInnis was amazingly cool reffing Game Four of the Conference Championship.

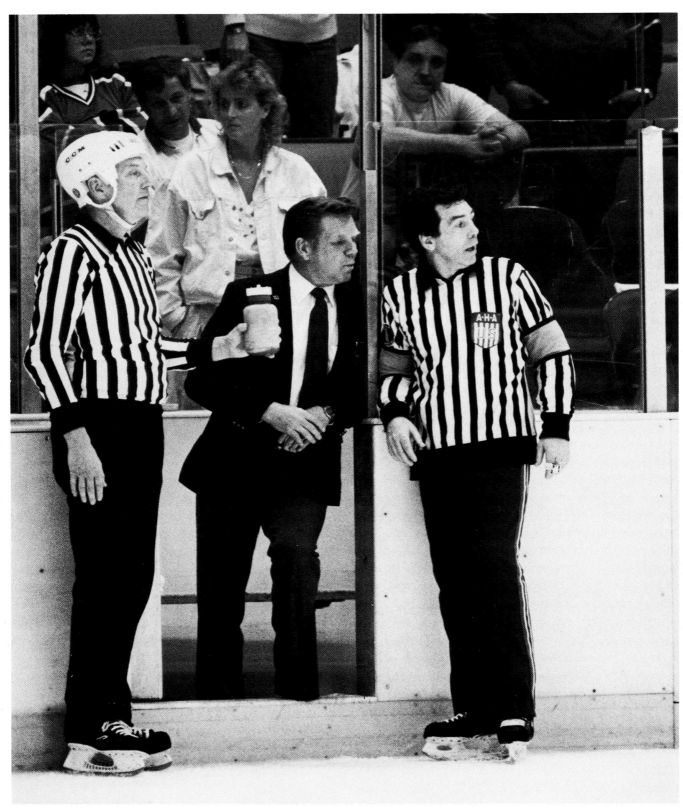

Replacement linesman Vin Godleski shares a breather with McInnis by the penalty box.

that substitute officials—each of whom had vast experience handling organized amateur league games—would be the best bet.

Of the New Jersey off-ice crew, those selected were Paul McInnis, a 52-year-old manager of the Murray Ice Rink in Yonkers; Vin Godleski, 51 years-old, and Jim Sullivan, a 50-year-old retired New York City policeman. McInnis and Godleski were off-ice officials at Byrne Arena while Sullivan worked at Nassau Coliseum in the same role.

Skates were found for all three. They donned yellow sweatshirts and took the ice one hour and six minutes after the scheduled start of the game. McInnis, who lives in Livingston, New Jersey, was designated the referee.

Although there was considerable skepticism among the audience as to how the replacement officials would stand up under the extremely tense conditions of a Wales Conference playoff game, to a man they did an extraordinary job. They were impartial, sharp, and rarely trailed the play.

The game itself belonged to the Devils, primarily because of Sean Burke's histrionics in goal. The Bruins could not blame the officiating; they took 33 shots at the 21-year-old rookie and he stopped all but one.

Burke got no favors from the substitute officials. Less than a minute into the game he was given a two-minute delay of game penalty by McInnis, but the Devils held off the foe and broke the ice at 10:47 when Claude Loiselle came up the middle on a three-on-one break, then dropped a pass to David Maley in the high slot. Maley faked defenseman Alan Pederson to the ice, cut to the circle and fired a shot that Lemelin kicked out but the rebound went in off a Bruins skate.

The time was 10:47, and within a minute the Devils had a two-goal lead. Pat Verbeek seized a bad clearing pass by Keith Crowder, moved in on Lemelin and sweetly deked him before pushing a backhander into the empty net.

After one period of play, the Devils led 2–0, and it was becoming apparent that McInnis, Godleski, and Sullivan were more than adequate for the occasion. Just in case, McCauley stationed himself in the penalty box and would offer advice from time to time, although the substitute officials seemed to have the situation well in hand.

The second period was not unlike any fiercely played Stanley Cup game. Tempers became frayed, and the players—not going out of their way to be more temperate for the sub-referee—high-sticked and fought as they are wont to do in a critical game. McInnis unhesitatingly dished out 48 penalty minutes which, in the end, provided Boston with a power play. That enabled Boston to get on the scoresheet. Craig Janney organized the play with a pass to Cam Neely, who cut across the crease and slipped the puck under Sean Burke's arm.

Because of the color of the jerseys originally worn by the amateur officials, some members of the media were describing the event as Yellow Sunday. However, regular black-and-white striped officiating jerseys were rushed to Byrne from South Mountain Arena in West Orange, New Jersey, the Devils' practice rink, and these were donned by McInnis, Godleski and Sullivan.

"By this time," kidded Sullivan, "we finally were getting used to the borrowed skates they had given us."

Tempers cooled as the third period unfolded. Nursing their one-goal lead, the Devils obtained a break when John MacLean moved from behind the Bruins' net out to the blue line. With a quick spin, he took a wrist shot that appeared to be sailing wide of the net until it bounced off defenseman Glen Wesley's pads. Brendan Shanahan seized the rubber and passed to Tom Kurvers who one-timed it past Lemelin. The time was 4:04.

From then on, the Devils played near-flawless hockey. "We rallied around Schony," said captain Kirk Muller. "He's done so much for our club that we're sticking with him. We believe he didn't push Koharski, and we're standing behind him. We stood up the best way we could."

Which was a 3–1 victory, tying the series at two apiece.

The post mortems were infinite. To a man, the Devils insisted that the episode inspired them to heights that might ordinarily have been unattainable. Even such a seemingly meaningless event as the pregame delay turned out—at least in the players' minds—to be an asset.

"The time when we were sitting and waiting helped us focus on what we had to do," said Burke. "We wanted to see Jim behind the bench, and it gave him a chance to talk about it. We used the delay to our advantage."

Unhappy though he was over the result, Sinden singled out Newell, Scapinello and Broseker for sharp criticism. "You can't walk away from the game," said the Bruins' leader.

McInnis, Godleski and, Sullivan were commended for their courage and willingness to take on an awesome task without any complaint despite unusual adversity. "For the first two periods," laughed Sullivan, "I had to use a whistle that came out of a box of Cracker Jacks."

Still, a feeling of uneasiness prevailed long after the final buzzer because all parties knew that the situation still was not fully resolved. In the meantime, the Devils celebrated their victory.

"It was a tough situation," said Tom Kurvers, "but we'll take the win. That was the primary goal. We'll take the win and go from here."

Ah, but where would the NHL go from here? Events in the next few days would be among the most momentous of the decade of the Devils.

13

CLOSE
BUT NO CIGAR

Over the weekend, the Devils had become a continent-wide story, front page in the United States and Canada with media descending on them in record numbers.

What concerned the Devils' high command more than anything was pure justice. The general staff was willing to accept a penalty if one was justified and if a hearing—which heretofore had been denied—was held.

It was freely assumed that if the NHL refused a hearing, as it had up until Monday, May 9, then the league would consider the Devils in the wrong. On the other hand, if the NHL reversed its position and offered to listen to the Devils' position, the Jerseyites would be vindicated.

On Monday afternoon, NHL spokesman Gary Meagher announced that the Schoenfeld suspension was rescinded. "We still don't think the initial order was invalid," said the league counsel Gil Stein, "but at

this point we're thinking a lot of things. By rescinding the suspension, we make last night like it never happened, but the matter under investigation still has to be concluded, and will be on Tuesday." A major question still to be answered had to do with the regular league officials. Would they remain on strike or would they return to work? And if they did return, would the NHL take any action against a group that sanctioned a walkout in the midst of the playoffs?

A meeting between league representatives and the NHL Officials Association was held in Toronto. A compromise was hammered out; the referees would resume working the rest of the playoffs but no penalty would be levied against them. The Devils could live with that, and, John Ziegler suddenly reappearing on the scene, the league convened a hearing for Schoenfeld to review his situation at Boston's Ritz-Carlton Hotel at 2 p.m. on Tuesday. It consumed

Despite a 7–1 loss, at least the focus returned to what was taking place on the ice.

almost three hours, after which Ziegler recessed the proceedings and announced that he would have a decision that day.

Within the hour Ziegler returned with the announcement that Schoenfeld was fined $1,000 and suspended for Game Five while the Devils also were fined $10,000.

Devils owner John McMullen said, "I disagree with the ruling completely."

At this point there was little else the Devils could do but regroup for the evening's match at Boston Garden. Lamoriello replaced Schoenfeld behind the bench and Burke was back in goal.

The Bruins scored two power play goals for a 2–0 lead before Brendan Shanahan cut the lead with a goal late in the period off a second rebound. A four-minute penalty to Boston late in the period gave New Jersey an excellent opportunity to get right back in the game. They couldn't get organized as the period ended and made no hay during

the three minutes and 43 seconds of power play in the second frame.

After that if was all Bruins. They scored five straight goals for a 7–1 decision.

To some witnesses to the contest, it marked the end of the Devils' season. "I don't think anybody in the hockey world thinks we'll be playing Boston in a seventh game," said Pat Conacher, "but we have some different thoughts on the matter. We'll show up for Game Six in Jersey and see what happens."

Game Six of the Wales Conference finals may not have been the best the Devils have ever played, but it certainly ranked with the most inspired. They took a heavy punch from the Bruins at 1:57 of the first period when Willi Plett beat Burke, but Schoenfeld's battlers refused to be demoralized.

"We knew we had to play our best game," said John MacLean, "because the Bruins wanted to get it over with."

Mark Johnson tied the score in Game Six.

The Devils desperately wanted to keep Boston from scoring a second goal before New Jersey got on the scoreboard. They assaulted the Bruins vigorously but without recompense until Mark Johnson tied the score at 15:40 of the period.

"You can take pressure two ways," said Johnson. "You can be hindered by pressure or you can be excited by it, and one of the reasons this team has done as well as it has is that we use it to lift and excite us." He added, "Pressure really hasn't bothered this team at all."

Especially not Johnson, who scored the goal to ensure that the Devils would not go to the dressing room trailing the Bruins as they had in the last game. Cirella started the play with a strong outlet pass from the Devils' end. The Bruins, showing the first signs of the sloppy play that would plague them all evening, were slow making a change.

Johnson opened fire on Lemelin from high in the slot, beating Lemelin who would not recover the poise he had shown throughout the five previous games.

But Johnson wasn't done yet, not even for the period. "Mark was skating about two inches off the ice tonight," said Schoenfeld after the game. "He's one of the players who can take charge all by himself."

His tenth playoff goal came with only 1:45 remaining in the period. After taking a feed from Sundstrom, Johnson beat Lemelin again from the slot, over the goalie's stick. Suddenly, the Bruins were trudging to the locker room down 2–1, shaking their heads and wondering why these upstarts from New Jersey wouldn't roll over and die as everybody predicted.

The second period brought about another strange event in a series already famous for unprecedented happenings. Having suffered through the hour long delay on Yellow Sunday, New Jersey fans were understandably hostile to the men wearing the striped shirts. A large sign behind the south goal read: "NJ shall overcome the Bruins-Ziegler refs." It was only a matter of time before Andy Van Hellemond and his crew became the target of the fans ire, and it happened nearly six minutes into period two when Claude Loiselle was called for a questionable penalty to give Boston a power play to aid their sagging spirits.

Like all great teams, the Bruins capitalized on the opportunity, with a Bob Sweeney power-play tally at 7:24. Moments before the rush that produced the goal, it appeared that Aaron Broten of the Devils had been hooked as Boston pulled out of their own zone, but no penalty was called. The fans responded by littering the ice with souvenir megaphones that had been dis-

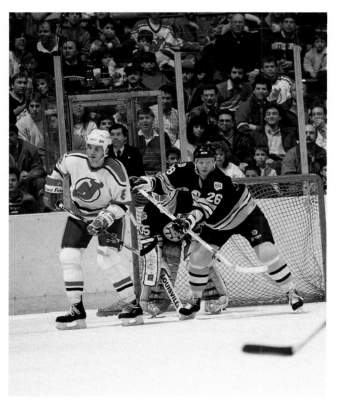

The Devils ignored the pressure in Game Six. Replacement ref Paul McInnis (background) had returned to his normal post as a goal judge.

tributed to them as they entered the arena. Van Hellemond and his crew left the ice, fearing for their safety. The veteran referee also sent the Bruins back to their dressing room to ensure that they wouldn't brawl with the Devils.

After a ten-minute delay, Doug Brown put the Devils back in the lead, with some brilliant help from linemates Pat Conacher and Andy Brickley. After Craig Wolanin dumped the puck into the left boards, it appeared that the Bruins' Glen Wesley would retrieve it easily. Conacher overtook Wesley, then crushed him into the boards, allowing the puck to slide behind the net, where Brickley was waiting. His quick centering pass to Brown ended in the rookie's 20-foot blast, beating Lemelin, who was on his way to a disastrous night. "I just don't think we had the killer instinct to put them away," said Wesley, who felt the Devils' killer instinct first-hand via Conacher's check.

Again the Bruins struck back, on a Michael Thelven goal at 14:17, only to see their hitherto excellent goalie look ridiculous three minutes later. "I know the bounces sure didn't go my way personally," agreed Lemelin in a post-game interview.

The play began, appropriately enough, with another apparent penalty that went unseen by the referee. John MacLean was hooked at Boston's blue line but continued up ice when no call was made. He carried in the puck all the way to the goal line and was nearly even with Lemelin when he wound up to shoot. The beleaguered Boston netminder failed to close the small space between his body and the post. The puck struck him behind the knee and ricocheted into the goal. "After that," a glum Lemelin said later, "you just start thinking it's not your night."

After he saw the puck go into the net, MacLean turned and shouted at Van Hellemond, then celebrated his sixth goal of the

Shanahan's words symbolized the team's inspired play.

Daneyko played some of the best hockey of his career as all the Devils' defensemen picked it up a notch.

period. The Bruins were stunned but undaunted, while the Devils were obviously believing what Shanahan had written on the chalkboard before the game, words he repeated with conviction after the victory: "A man's destiny is fulfilled not by chance, but by choice!"

"This was the most complete game we've played in the series," added MacLean, who had struggled under Carpenter and exploded after Schoenfeld took over, tallying clutch goals down the stretch and in the playoffs. "This was by far the best game for everybody."

Once again, the Devils would play a seventh game. "A lot of players have never been in Game Seven of any series," said a grateful Schoenfeld. "If you start training camp and someone said you'll be in Game Seven of the Stanley Cup semifinals, you wouldn't believe it."

The Bruins agreed, at least as far as the saying applied to the Devils, if not themselves. "We never thought the series would go seven games," admitted Bourque. "We thought we'd go back to Boston with the series behind us and the Stanley Cup ahead of us."

But the Devils, who had spent several weeks rewriting the book on great comebacks, never doubted that it would go to a seventh game.

"Nobody felt like the season was over," insisted Burke, who turned in another strong performance in goal. "Nobody felt like it was going to end tonight."

Conacher echoed Burke's sentiments. "Nobody in the hockey world thought we'd be going back to Boston," he said. "But there were 20 guys in the dressing room who thought we would."

There were also 20 guys in the Bruins' dressing room who were wondering if O'Reilly would start Lemelin in that game back in Boston.

series. It put the Devils ahead, 4–3, and proved to be the game-winner.

"He's been stoning us pretty good," admitted MacLean about Lemelin, who had twice in the series held New Jersey to one goal. "It gives us a lot of confidence, and we're going to shoot more."

When the Devils opened the third period with a goal by Conacher, who retrieved a loose puck in front of the net and beat Lemelin between his legs, O'Reilly had seen enough. New Jersey's five goals had come on 13 shots. He pulled Lemelin for Andy Moog, who made his first appearance since April 18. "I'm glad Andy went in," said Lemelin. "The way things were going, they could have had 20."

They ended up with only six, after Sundstrom added a final tally later in the third

"We can't blame the loss on Reggie," insisted Wesley. "You can't expect him to be great every night."

But could they expect him to be great one more night, after being shellacked so badly in game six? "I want to look at it with a positive attitude and bounce back from it. It's not the first time and it won't be the last." And, of course, Moog's appearance had been his first in weeks, and he had surrendered a goal, besides betraying some rink rust. His goals against average in three playoff games against Montreal was 4.33. All things considered, it had to be Lemelin.

And so it was—Lemelin vs. Burke. Game Seven at Boston Garden.

New Jersey hockey fans still shook their collective heads in disbelief that their once-twitted team had come so far, so fast.

There were no illusions about the coming test. Cramped Boston Garden hardly was a haven for visiting teams, and the Bruins had mastered its corners and tight center ice area as any good home team would. They would have a fanatical crowd roaring behind them, and, all things being equal, Terry O'Reilly would have them fully charged from the opening face-off. But the Bruins also had to come to the realization that the New Jersey foe was a serious challenger.

"They're for real," said Ken Linseman. "In the past few years their defense was kind of weak, but now it's tough, a real good group."

The finale was Game 100 of the Devils' stupendous season. Would there be more?

"I look at this simply as a one-game series," said Craig Wolanin. "Nobody has an advantage. It comes down to who's better mentally prepared. There's really not much more to say. We have to just go out there and do it."

Nobody can say they didn't try, although the demands were enormous. Handling the puck for the opening face-off was none other than referee Don Koharski. That the disputatious official would handle the game was known early that day, May 14, 1988, and it surprised even the foe.

"I thought they'd change it," said O'Reilly. "It was a very controversial point."

The Devils did not complain. They went out and played hockey. In the opening minutes they dominated Boston and finally seemed to have worked their way toward the opening goal.

Just three minutes and 41 seconds into the match, Kirk Muller skated around Bruins defenseman Michael Thelvin and fired from ten feet. Lemelin got his right pad on the drive but went to the ice and allowed the rebound to carom directly to Pat Verbeek who was camped exactly where he wanted to be, in front of the gaping four-by-six net.

To everyone in the audience and the millions watching the game on network and local television, it was a certain goal. Verbeek, who had led the Devils with 46 red lights over the season, couldn't possibly miss this grand opportunity. Verbeek figured, "Top shelf and it's in!" But there was one slight but significant problem—the puck and Verbeek momentarily hesitated in the hope that the rubber would become stabilized. So, here is the picture in one stopped frame: Lemelin was far to the right (his left) at the edge of the crease. Verbeek was on the open left (Lemelin's right) with the puck standing on its end. Lemelin's right hand, holding his stick, stretches back toward the emptiness of the middle of the net. Still, his move seemed hopeless.

Pat fired at the unencumbered opening and the puck sped goalward. Verbeek was poised to raise his stick in triumph. Devils rooters were about to come to their feet in a state of high glee.

At that point, the venerable Lemelin

chose to execute the save of his career by lunging across the crease.

Somehow—Reggie later called it "instinct that comes from years of experience"—he blocked the drive, deflecting the puck out of the air with his right arm. If there was a better save, the Devils couldn't imagine it. Verbeek stood transfixed in complete and utter disbelief. More than 14,000 throats in Boston Garden disgorged a high decibel roar, and when it finally subsided, the score was still 0–0.

Distraught but not destroyed, the Devils continued their assault and again thought for a split-second that they had at last gained the much-sought 1–0 advantage. This time is was Tom Kurvers who delivered a sizzling shot from the inside perimeter of the right circle after taking a delicious pass from the other side by John MacLean. Kurvers appeared to have Lemelin at his mercy, but, once again, the goaltender thwarted the drive and still the score was knotted at zero.

"Lemelin had a thought," observed Frank Brown in the *Daily News*, "'Look good early and your bench will be lifted.'"

The Devils were undaunted. They persisted but the two missed "sure" opportunities stung to the very core, and, gradually, the nervous Bruins regained their poise. They gained an advantage when Koharski made a questionable hooking call against the normally penalty-free Mark Johnson. With the power play in motion, Boston took a 1–0 lead when Craig Janney tipped Ray Bourque's shot past Burke at 8:59.

Smelling blood, the Bruins pounced on the opportunity, and three minutes later Moe Lemay deflected a Thelven shot into the net for a 2–0 Boston lead. That's the way the first period ended, but it was still all Bruins early in the second. Rick Middleton made it 3–0 at 2:57, beating Burke from

near the top of the right circle after Bourque had won the face-off from Claude Loiselle.

If the Devils were downhearted, you would never know it by their actions. They responded with more vim, vigor, and vitality and penetrated Lemelin's form at 15:28 of the second period on a goal by John MacLean. That made it 3–1 Boston at the end of two.

"We weren't finished with them," said Ken Daneyko, "not by a long shot."

Early in the third period, Daneyko took a vicious bodycheck but managed to move the puck into the left corner where MacLean and Bourque battled for possession. Meanwhile, Aaron Broten moved in and took possession, sending a pass to Kirk Muller whose ice-skimming shot from the slot beat Lemelin.

Now the Devils were only one behind with more than fifteen minutes remaining. They kicked their attack into an even higher gear and hurled a number of difficult shots at Lemelin. Several times Reggie looked vulnerable but managed to get in the way of the rubber.

They Jerseyites didn't succeed but they try, tried again—and again. It was still 3–2 when the clock had reached the twelve minute mark and the puck was cradled on Daneyko's stick. "All I wanted to do was make a move to the middle," the defenseman later lamented, and then . . ."

Unbeknownst to Daneyko, Craig Janney was lurking nearby. Anticipating the pass, Janney intercepted it on delivery and suddenly was in on a mini-breakaway against Burke. The goalie tried to poke check but the pool shot missed, Janney swung left, held on to the puck and slid it dead center into the net. It was 12:05 and 4–2 Bruins.

Try as they might, the Devils could not crank up a threatening offense again. The Bruins Cam Neely scored at 13:19, putting

As time ran out, the Devils accepted their fate.

the game out of reach. Linseman's open net goal at 19:36 was the final knot of the playoff package. Boston won the game, 6–2, and the series four games to three.

The Devils, who had made such beautiful music for two months, now sat exhausted in their dressing room listening to a requiem for their remarkable run.

"Most of our players had never known the thrill of winning a playoff series before this," said Schoenfeld, "and until tonight, most of them didn't know how much it hurts to lose one.

"I thought we might make a miracle of destiny comeback right up until the last 42 seconds. But, what can I say, the boys gave me everything they had and you really can't ask for anything more."

Downcast but still doughty, the Devils peeled off their sweat-drenched uniforms as the reporters descended on them for the last time this season. "You get on a roll," said Mark Johnson, "you start to believe it's never going to end. When it does, it hurts. It really does. You start to visualize it in the back of your mind. Everyone had thoughts of us carrying the Wales Conference Trophy around tonight, taking tomorrow off and going to Edmonton to meet the Oilers (Campbell Conference champions) on Monday."

A proud president-general manager Lou Lamoriello congratulated his men. Within a year of taking command of the organization, the Providence native had given the New Jersey hockey fans a most remarkable saga to cherish for the rest of their lives.

"Our club has proven," Lamoriello con-

As coaches and players met on the ice . . .

. . . respect was something the Devils' organization had gained throughout the NHL.

cluded, "that we no longer will be two easy points for every opponent. We have established our identity. The players believe they can win. I'd like people to still consider us underdogs, but I don't think they will."

Throughout the remainder of the spring and into the summer of 1988 the accomplishments of John MacLean, Sean Burke, Kirk Muller and friends would be discussed over barbecues at the beach and behind sports desks. "The Devils," boasted New York *Times* columnist Peter Vecsey, "were the first professional team proud enough to carry the name of the state of New Jersey

this deep into any playoffs."

Singling out THE outstanding note in the Devils' melody of a momentous year was difficult. Certainly, the sixth game win over the Islanders was one, not to mention the clincher against Washington. But when all was said and done, it came down to John MacLean's goal, beating Chicago in overtime which enabled the club to reach the playoffs for the first time ever.

"That," said Lamoriello, "was our Stanley Cup. That helped us sustain our focus. If you wrote a script, that made our organization. Anything we did from then on just solidified us."

The Devils raised a banner on opening night, but a repeat performance was not to be.

14

THE INEVITABLE LETDOWN

As the Devils savored the fruits of their delectable playoff dinner, the head chef, Lou Lamoriello, sounded a prophetic word of caution. "What often happens after a first-year player, or an organization that has success for the first time, gets to the second year is they think they don't have to prepare anymore. They forget what it took to attain that success. And they're in for a rude awakening."

It was an astute appraisal that would be echoed throughout the 1988–89 season, one that began with enormous hope at training camp in West Orange, New Jersey.

When the Devils gathered at South Mountain Arena at the start of September, 1988, nothing but hopeful sounds emanated from the training facility. "We accomplished something last year," said Ken Daneyko, "and now we expect to accomplish more."

Certainly, the lineup suggested bigger and better things. After his arresting rookie season, Sean Burke figured to be an imposing figure in goal while the defense had solidified and the attack now featured such big guns as John MacLean and Pat Verbeek, with captain Kirk Muller rapidly reaching his prime as both playmaker and team leader. With a season under his belt, Jim Schoenfeld loomed as a potential candidate for the Adams Trophy as coach of the year.

Media analysts were bullish about New Jersey. "The Patrick Division has a new team to worry about," asserted Barry Meisel of the *Daily News*. "The Devils were no Stanley Cup fluke."

An NHL preseason guide predicted a second-place finish. "Picking up where they left off last spring, the Miracle Devils will benefit from a full year of Sean Burke's goaltending, a young nucleus, and the leadership of Kirk Muller," it said.

The outlook, even by conservative estimates, was positive—and then the exhibition season began and, within weeks,

Despite limited playing time, Perry Anderson's all-out style made him a fan favorite.

doubts began to emerge.

After eight preseason games, the Devils had only two victories to show for themselves against five losses and a tie. In a game against Buffalo at The Meadowlands, they were walloped 11–3. Kurvers, of whom much was expected, was on the ice for six goals while Jack O'Callahan was on for five.

"Anything positive?" asked Schoenfeld in answer to a question. "Well, we had some good line changes. No one was seriously hurt and we have only one more exhibition game to go. That's about all I can say from a positive side."

The exhibition session sometimes is meaningful while other times it is completely meaningless. One never really knows until months have passed before making an appraisal of a sorry September. In the Devils' case, one could not obtain a good clue after the first three regular-season games.

After dropping the opener 4–1 at Philadelphia, New Jersey went to Quebec and beat *Les* Nordiques before returning to New York and the home opener for the Rangers at Madison Square Garden. On face value, it was a four-star event. Burke blanked the Broadway Blueshirts, 5–0 while Muller scored a pair of textbook, second-effort goals in a five-goal Devils third period.

It was the second shutout of Burke's 16-game regular career. He stopped 41 shots, nine during a four-minute power play. "When we played five-on-five," said the goalie, "we did pretty well."

One reporter predicted that Burke would be a top NHL goaltender for the next decade. Sean's sidekick, Bob Sauve, didn't disagree. "He was awesome," said Sauve. "The way Sean played, I don't think anybody could beat him."

Optimism was the order of the day as the Devils returned to New Jersey on October 14 for their home opener against the Montreal Canadiens. The result would demonstrate the unexpected top-to-bottom cartwheels a hockey team can experience in a season.

Burke gave up seven goals while his mates could score but three and MacLean's

THE INEVITABLE LETDOWN

Randy Velischek appeared in all 80 games in '89-90.

Tommy Albelin was plus-18 in 46 Devils' games after being acquired from Quebec in December following a serious leg injury to Driver.

two-goal effort was thoroughly obscured. Even worse, the Devils moved on to Washington where the Capitals put eight shots past Sauve to five for New Jersey, and then, as if to confirm the slump was for real, the Devils lost 4–0 to the Vancouver Canucks at Byrne.

Whew!

This was not the way Schoenfeld had hoped the script would evolve, but there would be little alteration until New Jersey beat the Rangers, 6–5, at The Meadowlands. Mark Johnson scored a pair, including the game-winner, to lift the Devils to the .500 mark (6–6–2). The club's aim was to clear the .500 plateau and establish the brand of supremacy they had exhibited the previous spring, from March through early May.

There were signs of hope. Road victories over Washington (6–3) and St. Louis (4–2) in mid-November put the club at 8–7–3. They had 19 points and sat in third place. It was a truly meaningful point because the Devils would never be above .500 again for the remainder of the season.

Back home against the Calgary Flames, the Devils had an opportunity to establish themselves firmly in a playoff position. A win over the big Smythe Division sextet would be just the spring to catapult them up to first place in the Patrick.

Instead, the Flames jumped on Burke for two first-period goals and were headed to a 5–3 victory over New Jersey. The Devils' power play was one-for-nine and, said Bruce Driver, "that was the difference."

That also was the end of the illusion that New Jersey would stay above .500. The loss to Calgary was followed by defeats at the hands of Washington, Philadelphia, and Calgary again. The Devils had dropped to 8–11–3 for 19 points and now were tied for fourth. Just two games later they would be in fifth place, from which they would never

climb for the rest of the season.

By the beginning of December, following a 5–3 home loss to Philadelphia, Schoenfeld began betraying his dismay with the club. "For the first time since I've been here," he said, "I see a lack of heart and desire for hard work. We analyzed certain aspects, and we realized guys are not working hard enough. There are guys who are not giving enough."

Asked whether the spring success might have been too much, too soon for the Devils, Schoenfeld replied, "I'll never say that it was a bad thing to make it to the semis last year, but our arms are so sore from patting each other on the back we can't shoot the puck anymore."

A heartening three-game winning streak early in January gave some solace to the faithful, but it was difficult to be sure which way the club was heading. "How should the Devils be judged?" asked John Dellapina of the Bergen *Record*. "Is a team's first-half record (14–19–7) a true representation of a talented group that lacks superstars? Or was last season's inspiring run to and through the NHL playoffs a better indication of the Devils' capabilities?

"The Devils' performance during the first half of the 1988–89 season hasn't been good. They are twelve points out of fourth place and the final Patrick Division playoff berth. That earns the Devils a C-minus midterm grade."

If New Jersey was to make the playoffs for the second year in a row, a late-winter rush would be necessary. After winning three out of four—including an 8–1 rout of Toronto—in February, the time was ripe for such a move.

A major vein of inspiration was the play of young Brendan Shanahan, who had melded neatly on a line with John MacLean and Patrik Sundstrom. "Brendan's skill level has risen to accomodate theirs," said

Schoenfeld of MacLean and Sundstrom.

Hope sprung eternal that the turnaround would happen. "We've done it before and we can do it again," promised Schoenfeld.

Unfortunately, the Devils fell prey to five consecutive losses when they could least afford them in mid-February. "We've been losing games we should have been winning," said Craig Wolanin. "It's coming back and slapping us in the face."

A spate of three wins out of four games in early March was the last rush the Devils could muster, and that wasn't enough to dislodge them from fifth place.

The disappointing season ended on April 2 with a 7–4 home win over Washington. New Jersey's final tally was 27–41–12, and it recalled the warning that Lamoriello had sounded at the beginning; hard work would be necesssary to retain the glow of March-April-May 1988.

"I knew we were in trouble in training camp," said Schoenfeld. "We were not prepared mentally or physically when we came to camp for this season.

"As the coach I am responsible. But the players have to share the responsibility. But I'll take the responsibility. I don't want the players to bear the burden of the season. Right from training camp, the hunger wasn't there. Not from everybody but from some players. Some players heard how terrific they were last season and rested on their laurels."

There would be no resting as far as Lou Lamoriello was concerned. He was determined to right the listing ship and already had begun the salvage job by preparing to obtain two of the best international players of contemporary hockey, Viacheslav Fetisov and Alexei Kasatonov.

The Year of The Russians was about to arrive.

15

THE RUSSIANS ARRIVE

The idea of importing international hockey stars to the NHL was not exactly a new one. Players such as Borje Salming and Anders Hedberg had demonstrated in the 1970s that the skill level of many stick-handlers on the other side of the Atlantic Ocean was equal — and sometimes superior — to their North American brethren.

But the scouting line stopped at the Iron Curtain. As long as the Cold War kept relations between the United States and the Soviet Union in a deep freeze, there was little hope that world class Russian players could strut their stuff wearing the colors of the Montreal Canadiens, Boston Bruins or, for that matter, the New Jersey Devils.

However, while most big-league hockey leaders assumed that the Cold War would remain a permanent fixture in global politics, one NHL owner thought otherwise. Dr. John McMullen of the Devils, through his international business interests, had a bet-

ter ear tuned to the political soundings than his colleagues and better insights as well.

At a time when other NHL clubs couldn't envision Russians playing major professional hockey, Dr. McMullen said, "Let's do it!" In 1983, a year after he purchased the Colorado Rockies and moved them to The Meadowlands, Dr. McMullen suggested to his general staff that they should draft Soviet players, presuming some good ones became available.

"My feeling," Dr. McMullen explained, "was that changes in the European political situation could come about and bring an easing of relations between East and West. If that happened, we might be able to lure a couple of players to the Devils. At least, it was worth a try."

At the June 1983 draft, much of the attention was focused on the Minnesota North Stars, who created a stir by selecting a Rhode Island high school star named

Who could have known that decisions enacted at the '83 draft table would yield MacLean, Terreri, Fetisov and Kasatonov.

Brian Lawton as the first overall pick. Considerably less fanfare greeted the Devils' move in the eighth round when they named defenseman Viacheslav Fetisov of the Soviet Union as their choice.

To many onlookers it represented an interesting but far-fetched choice. After all, who in his right mind figured the rival Russians would ever permit one of their stars to emigrate to America? The answer, of course, was very few. But Dr. McMullen was willing to be patient. "I didn't expect any of them to come immediately," he explained, "but there was a hope that, perhaps, in the future we might get lucky."

Actually, the Devils got lucky then and there in 1983. Not only were they able to

land Fetisov with the 150th pick overall, but on the 213th selection the name Alexei Kasatonov was added to the New Jersey list. Only a few, led by Dr. McMullen, filed away the choices for future reference. Devils beat writers were more concerned with their top banana, John MacLean, and Rhode Island-bred Chris Terreri who had come off a sensational season at Providence College.

Once the swirl of regular season play began the Russians were instinctively forgotten. There was hockey to be played, a new season to unfold, and a baby franchise to nurture. Likewise, Fetisov and Kasatonov had their own business on which to focus, primarily winning international championships for the Soviet Union.

Fetisov acknowledged the fans' ovation in January '89 appearance at The Meadowlands.

Fetisov and Starikov pull on Devils jerseys for the first time; they accept congratulations from team owner John McMullen.

But the winds of change began blowing ever so strongly in the land of Nikolai Lenin and Josef Stalin. The regime of Mikhail Gorbachev brought with it a warm liberalization that would forever change the political complexion of Mother Russia. By the time the 1988 Winter Olympics were being played in Calgary, terms like *glasnost* and *peristroika* had been introduced to the American lexicon.

Devils president Lou Lamoriello visited Calgary ostensibly to scout goaltending prospect Sean Burke but also to make contacts with Fetisov and Kasatonov. It had now become apparent that there was a light at the end of the sporting tunnel and the flicker was coming from Moscow.

Following New Jersey's miracle dash to a playoff berth and splendid performance in the Stanley Cup round, Lamoriello solidified his Russian contacts and made plans for a landmark visit to the Soviet Union. The immediate goal was to determine ways and means of unravelling the red tape that would secure the release of Fetisov. The long-range target was putting Slava and Alexei in the red, white, and green Devils uniforms.

Lamoriello realized that his mission to Moscow would require patience and fortitude. While *glasnost* was well and good for Gorbachev, there was the matter of Viktor Tikhonov to consider. Like any commander, Tikhonov, the leader of Soviet hockey, was not the least bit tickled pink over losing two of his most formidable performers. And there were others in Russia who frowned on the idea of losing two world class defenders.

"I didn't harbor any illusions that it would happen just like that," said Lamoriello, "but, as the saying goes, you have to take the first step if you're going to walk the mile."

Lamoriello was right; it didn't happen "just like that." The process of gaining clearance for Fetisov was long and often agonizing. It involved the Soviet Ice Hockey Federation and the Russian Army, among other obstacles. After all, Slava was officially a major in the Soviet armed forces, and, even in enlightened Russia, you just don't walk away from your military obligations until a number of bureaucratic gates are lifted.

By this time the media had grabbed the Devils-Russians story and was running with it with typical journalistic fervor. In doing so, the public became riveted to the unfolding saga and concomitantly impatient for the deal to be done. But the Russians were in no rush and the 1988-89 season began and ended without any signings.

There was, however, a sighting; Fetisov's Central Red Army team played an exhibition with the Devils at Byrne Arena. In an adroit strategic-diplomatic maneuver, Lamoriello invited Yuri Dubinin, the Soviet Ambassador to the United States, to drop the first puck, along with U.S. Deputy Secretary of State John Whitehead and Dr. McMullen.

Aware of the sensitive problem of turning Fetisov into a permanent Devil, Dubinin asked Slava if he genuinely wanted to play in New Jersey. When the reply was enthusiastically in the affirmative, Dubinin assured Fetisov that he would cable Soviet authorities and hasten the process.

Devils captain Kirk Muller attempted to accelerate the social process by personally welcoming the defenseman to Byrne Arena. "I hope," said Muller, "that one of these days we'll be teammates."

Everyone knew that the collaboration would not take place in the 1988-89 season, so now the focus was on the spring of 1989. By the time the June draft had come and gone, all of the necessary elements were in

Dimitri Lopuchin (on players' left) served as interpreter and helped greatly with the cultural adjustment.

place. On July 7, 1989, the media were summoned to Byrne Arena's Winners Club for THE press conference.

At long last, the Russians were here!

There was, of course, Viacheslav Fetisov, who had been the principal object of Lamoriello's pursuit. Accompanying him was a barrel-chested fireplug-type comrade named Sergei Starikov who also manned the blueline but was hardly known to American hockey people.

Surely, the two proudest individuals in the jammed restaurant were Dr. McMullen and Lamoriello. The Devils' owner at long last was seeing his foresight tangibly

rewarded, whereas the club's president and general manager was enjoying the fruits of those tedious — but nonetheless essential — negotiations that would have frustrated a lesser executive.

"It was a long battle," said Dr. McMullen with an expansive grin, "but better late than never."

Fetisov and Starikov were flanked by Devils conditioning coach Dimitri Lopuchin, who speaks fluent Russian. Lopuchin fielded the endless questions and translated for the pair. The flock of television and radio crews as well as the print media couldn't get enough of them. Slava and Sergei

Lou Lamoriello's unyielding behind-the-scenes effort made the whole thing possible.

happily obliged—with a lot of help from Dimitri.

Many of the questions, quite naturally, zeroed in on the potential problems of acclimatizing to American life. Apparently, this would not be a dilemma for Slava's beauteous blonde wife, Lada. Days earlier she had discovered the wonders of Saks Fifth Avenue. As for the NHL, Fetisov seemed less concerned than his questioners. "Hockey is hockey," he observed. "You play and you react to situations accordingly. There's no point in complaining or mixing words."

There were no complaints and only kind words throughout the gala gathering. Coach Jim Schoenfeld asserted that both players were experienced in international competition and were not likely to be fazed by the ambience of the NHL. "I have no doubt that Fetisov will fit neatly into our plans," said Schoenfeld. "For years he demonstrated that he's a leader on and off the ice."

Starikov was another story. His talents were obviously more limited and there remained some question as to whether he had the overall ability to make the team. This and other questions would be answered when the firing actually began.

Before the actual baptism of fire on

Fetisov picked up a power-play assist on his first NHL shift at The Spectrum.

The team's glut of defensemen made it tough for off-season signee Reijo Ruotsalainen to find ice time.

opening night, there was a matter of training camp to conquer. While Fetisov was virtually guaranteed a place on the varsity, there would be significant competition. Such young veterans as Ken Daneyko, Bruce Driver, Tom Kurvers, Craig Wolanin, Randy Velischek, and Tommy Albelin were approaching their prime, not to mention recently-signed Reijo Ruotsalainen and American League Olympian prospect Eric Weinrich.

Both Fetisov and Starikov prevailed. Slava impressed in many ways but most of all with his radar-like passes that catapulted forwards on to the attack. "It's amazing how well he sees a play develop," observed former Devil Peter McNab during a pre-season scrimmage at South Mountain Arena. "Slava will just need a little time to learn the styles of his teammates — and vice versa."

Fetisov's primary problem was that he had become accustomed over the years to retain control of the puck a lot longer than defensemen normally do in the NHL game. As a result, he was susceptible to zealous forechecking. The question surrounding Starikov was simply whether or not he had the legs to keep up with big-league speed.

The answers were supplied, in part, on October 4, 1989, when Slava and Sergei skated out onto the forbidding ice at Philadelphia's Spectrum. Opening night had arrived and a very special aura of anticipation gripped not only the New Jersey players but the 17,000-plus fans who had filled the Flyers' home rink.

Externally intimidating, the Broad Street Bullies were expected to harass the Soviets and thoroughly disrupt the Devils' game plan. But the intimidation tactics immediately backfired. Within a minute, Flyers enforcer Craig Berube was slapped with a two-minute roughing penalty, and Slava was dispatched to the right point to quarterback the power play.

What followed seemed to be a maneuver right out of a "How To" guide. Muller forechecked, gained the puck, slid a pass to Fetisov, and Slava immediately released his shot. The puck hit New Jersey's Sylvain Turgeon in the chest and ricocheted into the net.

It was 5–0 Devils before the game was half over. At times Fetisov appeared somewhat disoriented by the ebb and flow of NHL hockey, but, for the most part, his superior skills prevailed. Starikov's overall puck sense kept him competitive although he was burned on one breakaway. When the dust had cleared, New Jersey owned a persuasive 6–2 victory. The Russians had come, had seen, and had conquered.

"I was impressed with the concentration that is necessary," Slava opined in the victor's dressing room. "There's little time to relax because play moves about so quickly."

And, besides, one game does not a season make. Nevertheless, the critical acclaim for that one performance was enough to please Dr. McMullen and Lamoriello. Fetisov was praised for his extraordinary passing while Starikov, in the view of one media observer, "showed he belonged."

In order to find room for Fetisov and Starikov, adjustments had to be made in the Devils' lineup. Craig Wolanin, Ken Daneyko, and Tom Kurvers were alternately benched as Schoenfeld sought the proper blend while the Russians worked their way into the flow. Events would prove that the road ahead, to say the least, would be riddled with potholes.

The opening game euphoria was tempered by a 4–4 tie with the Penguins at home followed by a disappointing 4–2 loss to Calgary before the Jersey fans. Inter-

estingly, the element that seemed to be threatening the Russians—NHL rough play—hardly surfaced as the Devils headed for the first post in the regular-season race. But by the time Game Nine of the campaign was over with, the issue of violence toward the Soviets became a *cause-celebre*.

The time bomb exploded at Maple Leaf Gardens in Toronto on October 23, 1989, after the Devils had soared into a 5–2 lead early in the second period. Toronto, now coached by Doug Carpenter, had become notorious for aggressive play. Trailing by three, the Leafs began taking runs at the Devils, culminating with Dan Daoust clipping Sean Burke in the New Jersey crease. A Pier Sixer erupted that featured a bout between Burke and his opposite Mark Laforest.

As the hitting mounted, the Maple Leafs shortened the scoring gap to a point where the result now was in doubt. The critical episode in question developed when Fetisov moved behind his net. Rambunctious Wendel Clark nailed Slava along the boards and then, without rhyme or reason, pummeled the Russian about the head. Fetisov appeared more stunned than injured. "I never expected him to do that," Slava later explained. "It just didn't occur to me that he would start swinging."

That was the bad news. The good news was New Jersey emerged with a 5–4 victory and had established itself as a competitive club with—unlike the previous year—distinct playoff possibilities. However, the future would depend on how Fetisov emerged from the first incident of his NHL career.

Toronto papers made much of the Clark confrontation and the fact that Schoenfeld had benched Slava for the final minutes of the game. Fetisov was chided for not retaliating against Clark, and even members of the media began taking sides on the

John Cunniff proved to be extremely popular with the players.

issue as the Devils headed for Calgary and a match with the Flames at The Saddledome.

Fetisov was eagerly anticipating the opportunity to skate against his old pal, Sergei Makarov, and 19,990 Calgary fans were looking forward to seeing the Devils' Russian in action. Instead, Schoenfeld, who seemed to be overreacting to the Toronto incident, chose to bench Slava. The ploy appeared to anger more than inspire the defenseman and the loss to Calgary did little to enhance Schoenfeld's stature.

After 14 games, the Devils sported a 6–6–2 record which did not seem consonant with the roster's talent. Their second place position was a bit deceptive in that they were 0–2–1 in their last three games and skating on a treadmill. Persuaded that quick action was necessary, Lamoriello replaced

Schoenfeld with assistant coach John Cunniff.

Some critics suggested that Schoenfeld was sacrificed to appease Fetisov but this hardly was the case. Lamoriello was trying to ice a winner, and if a Soviet did not play up to his standards, you could bet that the Russian would go; which is precisely what happened to Starikov. By late December it was concluded that Sergei would benefit from more ice time in the minors, and he was dispatched to Utica of the American League.

It was the Devils' good fortune to finally gain clearance for their other 1983 draft choice, Alexei Kasatonov, an eight-time Soviet League All-Star. After a brief shake-down cruise around the AHL, Kasatonov was promoted to the big team at the start of

Alexei Kasatonov arrived at Christmas and seemed to fit right in.

1990 and made his New Jersey debut on January 4, 1990, against Wayne Gretzky and the Los Angeles Kings.

Tall and graceful—seemingly smiling at all times—Kasatonov stepped into the lineup without missing a beat. "He'll be an asset," said Cunniff, "and, make no mistake, he can handle the rough play."

He could also handle Gretzky, as the 4–2 final score indicated. Alex, as he quickly became known to the media and teammates, worked the power play, killed penalties and took a regular turn. "From what I could see," said Gretzky, "Kasatonov doesn't look a bit out of place in the NHL."

Nor in the Devils' locker room. Teammates took to Alex's easy-going nature and even though he had difficulty with the language—when Dimitri Lopuchin wasn't around—Kasatonov was more than eager to be "one of the boys."

Eventually, Cunniff united Fetisov and Kasatonov as they had been on the Soviet national teams. Not surprisingly, they blended well, and just past the mid-point of the season, the Devils had climbed to first place. There were some memorable wins along the way, especially a 4–2 triumph over the Penguins at Pittsburgh's Civic Arena. John MacLean paced the New Jersey attack with a shorthanded and even-strength goal while Doug Brown and Patrik Sundstrom rounded out the attack.

Some analysts regard that game as Fetisov's finest up to this point; he was on the ice for all four Devils scores, assisted on two goals, blocked a pair of shots, and rebounded from a Mario Lemieux blindsider without a whimper. Lemieux was frustrated since Slava had blanketed *le Grand Magnifique* all night.

A quiet concern to the Jersey general staff was the manner in which Fetisov and Kasatonov would handle the homestretch. Neither had ever experienced the incessant pounding of an 80-game schedule nor the mounting pressure of a March playoff run in the Patrick Division. As the other clubs prepared for ther final drive, each of the six teams had a chance for a playoff spot. It was evident that the Russians would make or break the Devils' chances.

On March 2 each contributed significantly in another game against Pittsburgh, this time at Byrne Arena. The Devils prevailed, 6–5, and both Alexei and Slava delivered pivotal goals. "It was a very important win for us," Fetisov allowed when it was over. "We know there's little margin for error."

Wendel Clark made that discovery when he returned to Byrne Arena for Round Two of the much-discussed rivalry with Fetisov in January. As expected, the game was intensely played but the unknown was whether Slava would challenge the Toronto toughie.

The answer was provided in the third period when Clark carried the puck along the right boards. Fetisov, who was in the right defense position—diagonally across the ice from Clark—suddenly wheeled toward the Maple Leaf.

Without realizing that he had become a target, Clark accelerated past center ice by which time Fetisov bore down on him full speed ahead. However, a split-second before the impending collision, Clark caught sight of Slava out of the corner of his eye and applied the emergency brakes. Fetisov kept coming and made contact—although less than expected—with the Leaf. Wincing with pain, Clark nevertheless returned to the fray and was hit again, cleanly, by the Russian.

Clark dropped his gloves and this time Fetisov followed suit, but before the Devil could make a move Wendel dropped him with a right cross. The blow required repairs, but as soon as the stitches were

Bruce Driver's strong comeback season was overshadowed somewhat by the Soviet story.

Sylvain Turgeon scored 30 goals in his only season with New Jersey.

taken Fetisov scrambled back onto the ice and finished the game with a flourish. Clark was finished for the season—Fetisov's check had sufficiently damaged his knee to render him *hors de combat*.

The Devils had one more game left in Toronto, on February 17, and despite the enormous build-up—The Toronto *Sun* ran a WANTED! poster with a Fetisov photo— Slava had handled himself with aplomb. Unfortunately, his club was not winning enough hockey games. The Devils had slipped out of first place and had plummeted to fourth. Just two days before the trade deadline (March 6) their record was a disappointing 27–31–8 for 62 points.

Shortly before the deadline Lamoriello dealt Jim Korn to Calgary for a fifth-round draft pick and followed that with a blockbuster; former first-round pick Craig Wolanin and a player to be named later—

which turned out to be Randy Velischek— were dealt to Quebec for future Hall of Famer Peter Stastny. Whether coincidence or otherwise, the Devils responded with a 2–1 home win over St. Louis and followed that with a 4–2 triumph over the Islanders. Stastny's positive effect became more apparent with every game. When his former Nordiques teammates came to New Jersey on March 10, Stastny was a dominant force in a 9–3 victory.

It was now mid-March and the finish line was in sight. Aided by Stastny, the Devils had reached the .500 mark with 32 wins, 32 losses, and eight ties. They were six points out of first place and smiling. "We've found the groove again," said David Maley who more and more was becoming an effective checking forward. "If all goes well, we should make the playoffs and maybe even finish first."

But all did not go well. A March 20th home loss to the Flyers was a traumatic blow mostly because the Philadelphians were a team New Jersey *had* to beat out for a playoff berth and nothing went right for Cunniff's troops in the 3–2 loss. Every team — including Philadelphia, Pittsburgh and the Islanders — had a chance to pass the Devils.

If New Jersey had the goods, it would be determined by the weekend ahead; starting at The Spectrum and finishing at Buffalo's Auditorium, following a weekday night game at Chicago.

The scenario started scarily. The Blackhawks spanked the Devils 6–3, making the

Peter Stastny provided a lift down the stretch.

weekend challenge even more daunting. Part I took place on March 20 at The Spectrum. If New Jersey lost, their lead over Philadelphia would dwindle to a point. And it looked like that was what would happen. Ken Linseman put the Flyers ahead 1–0 early in the first period but Peter Stastny soon tied the score. Then Alexei Kasatonov set up John MacLean with the go-ahead goal, and the Devils never relinquished the lead, en route to a 5–2 decision. Both Kasatonov and Fetisov played like All-Stars.

Part II took place in Buffalo a day later. This time New Jersey jumped into a 4–1 lead and held it into the third period. Then the Sabres counterattacked and reduced the score to 4–3 with five minutes remaining. In the final minute, Buffalo pulled goalie Clint Malarchuk and gained two vital face-offs in the Devils' end. The visitors held fast until only a dozen seconds remained when Sabres defenseman Grant Ledyard unleashed a mighty blast that was headed goalward — until Fetisov smothered the shot with his hurling body and the Devils had two more pivotal points.

The victory ensured New Jersey of a play-off berth, and now they took aim at second place. A midweek 4–1 win over Washington took care of that. Suddenly, the Devils had taken on the trappings of a serious Stanley Cup contender. Although the Rangers had clinched first place, it was New Jersey that resembled the Patrick Division's best on March 29. The home crowd was treated to a 6–4 triumph and a truly marvelous performance by Fetisov. Slava was in on all but one Devil goal and looked more dominating than at any time in his young NHL career.

"Slava is comfortable in the NHL," said a satisfied Cunniff. "He and Alex have given us a nice foundation on defense."

For Cunniff & Co. the regular season would end the following night at Boston Garden. If they could produce one point it

Brendan Shanahan posted a then-career-high 30-goal, 72-point season in '89-90.

would mean a new franchise record for points. New Jersey was 37–34–8. In 1987-88 they had gone 38–36–6 for 82 points.

But the Bruins were giving nothing away. They nursed a 3–2 lead down to the game's final minute. With 26 seconds left, Bruce Driver drilled home the tying goal and a new team mark of 83 points had been established. New Jersey ended its 80-game campaign with a tie, a record, and pride in a job well done.

In the critical homestretch the Devils went 5–0–1. Their overall closing streak was a commendable 13–5–1, and for that they could thank Slava, Alexei and Peter, among many others.

Fetisov and Kasatonov had more than justified Dr. McMullen's 1983 decision to draft them and Lamoriello's painstaking trips to the Soviet Union. The Soviets had neatly melded into the team fabric. "When Alex and Slava got going," said David Maley, "that's when the rest of us followed suit."

As everyone who has watched hockey realizes, the playoffs, as they say, "are a whole new ball game." This would be a new experience for the Soviets, who had been accustomed to pressure cooker situations but never the Stanley Cup round.

"It's reasonable to assume that the Soviets will be geared up for the playoffs," said Lamoriello. "Every indication that we've seen is that they play better in the more important games. There has been some unevenness in their play, but when the playoffs come around, we hope that gets better. The one thing we have to worry about is the short time between the end of the regular season and the start of the play-offs. I don't think they're used to a quick turnaround like that."

The president-general manager was pro-phetic, to say the least. No question, the first 80-game schedule of their lives had taken a toll on Fetisov and, to a lesser extent

(remember Kasatonov came to the team in mid-season) his partner. Still, as they pre-pared for third-place Washington in the opening playoff round, there was absolutely no way to determine how the comrades would handle post-season play.

Overlooked by many as the series got underway was the fact that the Capitals had beaten the Devils in their regular season series, four games to three. Washington specialized in tight-checking, hard-hitting hockey and would rush the Devils from the very outset.

Game One at Byrne Arena hardly was a defensive classic. Down 2–0 in the first period, New Jersey fought the uphill battle over three periods and managed to come out of regulation with a 4–4 tie. The edge the Devils had hoped to gain was not to be attained. The ubiquitous Dino Ciccarelli completed his three-goal hat trick beating Sean Burke at 5:34 of the first overtime period.

Game Two also was out of character for both clubs. Defense was sacrificed for attack, and a surplus of goals was the result. At various points the score was 2–2, then 4–4, and eventually 6–4 for the Devils late in the third period, until Ciccarelli caused some heartburn with another Washington tally.

In the final minute Caps coach Terry Murray pulled out all stops — including goalie Mike Liut — and threw a total offense at Chris Terreri in the Devils' net. The little guy stopped everything until a last, desper-ate Washington drive appeared to be sailing over his shoulder. At that moment Fetisov's hand emerged and deflected the puck out of harm's way. The Devils had tied the series at one apiece on the strength of a 6–5 win.

Fetisov described his critical thrust as "my volleyball save." Kasatonov was lauded for his steady play and the Devils departed for Washington with a new confidence that they could turn the series in their favor.

That they did was somewhat surprising considering that Cunniff's crew managed only ten shots on goal over three periods. Still, New Jersey scored twice and Terreri — starting his second straight game — thwarted all but one Washington scoring attempt. The Devils led the series two games to one and appeared ready to take the opening round away from Washington.

Inexplicably, Cunniff broke up his winning combination and replaced Terreri with Burke for Game Four. For nearly half the game it looked like a good move. The teams were deadlocked at 1–1 until John Druce got the go-ahead goal for the Caps. Washington got another in the third period. The final score was 3–1, and the series was tied at two apiece.

Cunniff went back with Terreri when the teams returned to Byrne Arena for Game Five, but Washington now had the momentum and edged the Devils 4–3. The Capitals not only had the lead but Game Six would be at Capital Centre on April 15.

Any thoughts by the home folks that the Devils would lie down and die were dissipated early in the first period when New Jersey repulsed a Washington power play with ease. Just as it ended Kasatonov stepped out of the penalty box to find the puck in his lane and nobody between Alexei and Washington goalie Don Beaupre.

Taking a gamble, Beaupre burst from his crease and tried to outrace the Russian for the lost puck. Kasatonov got there first and found himself along the left boards with a gaping net 25 feet away. Sensing that another Washington player would be closing in on him, Alexei decided to take the shot rather than move into better scoring position. As it happened, it was the wrong move. The shot skimmed too far to the left, harmlessly hit the outside of the net and left the score tied, 0–0.

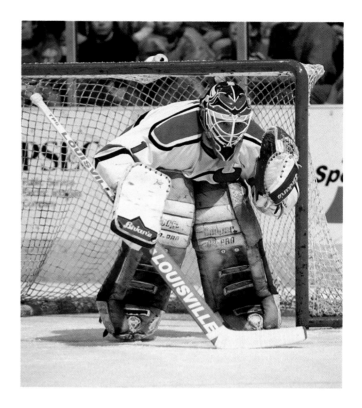

While Sean Burke was the main man during the regular season, Chris Terreri played four of six in the playoffs and had emerged as a contender for the number-one job.

Unfazed, the Devils mounted a string of attacks — Kirk Muller and Fetisov each had splendid opportunities — but could not beat Beaupre. With less than a minute remaining Washington's Steve Leach capitalized on a Devils defensive error and beat Terreri. The Capitals scored again in the second period to open a 2–0 lead, but John Mac-Lean got one back to reduce the lead to 2–1. But again the Caps made good on a last-minute thrust and exited with a 3–1 lead.

Still, the Devils wouldn't toss in the towel. Stastny rallied them with five minutes gone in the third to make it a 3–2 game. From that point on the Devils did everything but tie the game. Stastny had an exceptionally good chance to tie the game with a minute left but couldn't control a bouncing puck and Washington ran out the clock for the 3–2 win and the series victory.

While the defeat was distasteful — what losses aren't? — the Devils emerged from the 1989-90 season secure in the knowledge that their Russian experiment was a success. While something less than All-Stars, Fetisov and Kasatonov both had played nobly overall and figured to improve now that they had their rookie NHL seasons under their belts.

There were a number of other positives. Brendan Shanahan was gradually maturing into a top-flight offensive force; John Mac-Lean had become one of the most feared sharpshooters in the league; David Maley looked better every month; Bruce Driver was one of the NHL's most underrated backliners, and Peter Stastny had given the New Jersey power play an added dimension.

Further, there was the coming-of-age of Chris Terreri. Once regarded as nothing more than a second-stringer, Terreri figured prominently in the Devils' homestretch run and was the winner of New Jersey's two playoff games.

Sure, it would have been wonderful to have knocked off Washington but, all things considered, the Devils could find much to be satisfied about when all was said and done in 1989-90. Certainly, it was enough to provide optimism for the first full season in the new decade of The Nineties.

16

A HECTIC PATRICK DIVISION RACE

The 1989-90 season had its virtues. The team made the playoffs after a letdown the year before, proving that 1988's playoff berth was not a fluke, and that the team would not return to the mediocrity of the early seasons. But that fact hardly mattered to New Jersey fans, who could never be pleased by simply making the playoffs after having seen their team reach the seventh game of the Wales Conference finals two years before.

Neither the players nor the front office could blame the team's failure on youth or inexperience—nor did they wish to do so. Entering their eighth season with a solid core of talent led by exemplary captain Kirk Muller, the Devils were actually being called underachievers after their first-round loss to Washington.

Lamoriello would certainly agree that his team was talented, but he attributed their early playoff exit to a lack of size rather than a lack of desire. He lauded the work ethic of Muller, promising John MacLean, and young Brendan Shanahan, but against the close-checking, clutching style of the Caps, his team had been overwhelmed and their superior skill smothered.

The G.M.'s first move to add size and strength up front was a typically bold one. He traded Sylvain Turgeon, a high-scoring but physically reticent winger, to Montreal in exchange for Claude Lemieux, a hard-hitting grinder who could also go to the net. In three full seasons with the Canadiens, he never registered less than 27 goals, while infuriating opponents with a busy stick and an even busier mouth. "Adding Lemieux gives us a dimension which we may have lacked at times last year," explained the G.M.. "He's a solid player who can simultaneously contribute to our offense and eliminate the opposition's ability to take liberties with our players." Added Lamoriello, "Being able to bring in a player like Claude on the eve

Lemieux delivered everything the team could have asked for in his first season as a Devil.

of training camp is great from all standpoints."

Few people in Montreal would agree. As Hugh Delano noted in the New York *Post*, the Habs would probably have traded him for a sack of pucks. For all his talent, the tough winger had drawn the ire of teammates, coaches, the front office, and many fans. The accusations ranged from outright laziness and being a "bad influence" to faking injuries and taking repeated stupid penalties. He had publicly feuded with management, who had alternately fined and suspended him to no avail. The Canadiens were happy to acquire Turgeon but far happier to be rid of Lemieux.

Lamoriello's next deal involved another player who was at odds with his team. Veteran Laurie Boschman, who also combined a scoring touch with physical play, had

repeatedly stated his desire to get out of Winnipeg. The Devils were more than happy to oblige him, in exchange for ex-Ranger forward Bob Brooke. "Looking at our three centers," Lamoriello noted, "Laurie is a different type of player. He's one of the better face-off men and, quite frankly he's just ruined us," added Lamoriello, referring to Boschman's seven goals and twelve assists in nineteen games against the Devils.

Another physical presence was Troy Crowder, a 6'4", 215-pound right wing who had been brought up from Utica late in the previous season to add muscle to the Devils' lineup. After battling the Capitals' John Kordic to a draw in the playoffs, he earned a spot on the roster for 1990-91. He would play on the Devils' checking line with Boschman and Al Stewart, another scrapper who also killed penalties.

Coach Cunniff, entering his first full season behind the Devils' bench, was optimistic in training camp. "There was competition among the players to see who would be in the best shape reporting to camp," he revealed. "They challenged each other in that, and it showed me they had made a commitment to the team and the season."

Perhaps nobody was more committed than the team's two Soviets, Fetisov and Kasatonov, who were anxious to improve their play now that they had NHL experience. "Overall, I think he had a pretty good year," the coach stated. "But if I know Slava, he probably wasn't satisfied, and he wants to play better this season."

If there was one obvious chink in the Devils' armor, it was the prospect of losing forward Walt Poddubny, whose ailing knee required reconstructive surgery. Poddubny would miss the entire season, as he had in '89-90. Another concern was goalie Sean Burke's sore back, which caused him to miss some preseason, though he was

Laurie Boschman had a solid year and excelled in the playoffs while shadowing Lemieux.

Walt Poddubny's offensive skills remained intact, but his back and knee refused to do the same.

expected to start in goal on opening night. "I like this team," Cunniff asserted. "I'm confident going into the season with the talent we have. We'll be a physical team," he maintained, "and we have high expectations. We have to live up to them."

Burke was indeed the goalie on opening night, but he wasn't the story of the Devils' 3–3 tie with Detroit. The game made Lamoriello look like a genius. Lemieux was a dynamo from the moment he took the ice, scoring the Devils' first two goals of the season, and banging people all over the ice. But the real test came when the Red Wing's Bob Probert responded by mugging Lemieux, who hit the ice hard and had to be helped back to the bench.

For the Devils, it was imperative that they not allow Probert's tactics go unpunished. Al Stewart went after the much larger Red Wing and was soundly beaten, though his

display of courage in challenging the league's heavyweight champ did not go unnoticed.

But it was Crowder who could best deal with Probert. He challenged the Red Wings' enforcer, who had not lost a fight in years. Crowder was obviously unimpressed and unintimidated. He overpowered Probert, jerked him off balance, pulled his jersey over his head and pummeled him with a series of right hands. When he pulled the jersey completely off, Probert was bleeding from a gash under his eye which required stitches.

"I think it picked us up," said Crowder, refusing to boast. "It's always nice to know somebody's watching out for you."

Lemieux, the victim of Probert's blind-side attack, returned to the game later. He agreed with his teammate. "When Troy did what he had to do," he said, "it lifted us as a team, gave us a spark."

The final spark was the tying goal by Shanahan with fifteen seconds remaining. The only negative note was an injury to John MacLean, who suffered a concussion after a vicious check by Lee Norwood.

After a victory over another very aggressive opponent, the Philadelphia Flyers, the Devils dropped their first game of the season to Pittsburgh, 7–4. This game, as much as any other, exemplified what would be New Jersey's problem throughout the season. The team was woefully inconsistent, not only from week to week or even game to game, but from one period to the next. After going ahead 3–1 with a strong defensive-minded approach, they completely collapsed, allowing six goals, three of which came in the third period.

"We were playing great, but we kept them in it, and they barraged us," admitted Ken Daneyko, one of the beleaguered defensemen. Four penalties in the third period also hurt New Jersey, as did the fact that Pittsburgh's tying goal went in off of Devils defenseman Bruce Driver.

"That kind of goal is deflating, and it switches momentum," remarked Cunniff, "then there's a lull after it and they get two quick goals." Chris Terreri had started in goal, making 30 saves and looking impressive until the late assault overwhelmed him. "I really thought we had won it," he said. "They just came at us real hard."

But the Devils rebounded and continued to play hard in their own right. Nobody was pushing the Devils around anymore. Crowder demolished two of Philadelphia's best fighters, Jeff Chychrun and Tony Horacek, in one game at the Spectrum. Chychrun left with a broken nose, and the Devils raised their record to 4–1, and were still undefeated at home.

But the team was already displaying its tendency to go from brilliance to medi-

ocrity with no rhyme or reason. A 5–3 victory over Calgary was a truly superior effort, with Laurie Boschman scoring two goals in addition to his typical strong defensive game. "I played in that division a number of years," Boschman recalled with confidence; "I've scored my fair share of goals against them."

Terreri, playing for an ailing, struggling Burke, yielded three goals in the third period but rebounded to preserve the win. "They got a couple of breaks," he explained. "When we played within the framework of our game, we played well."

Most encouraging of all was a tough 3–2 victory over playoff nemesis Washington, which seemed to further demonstrate the

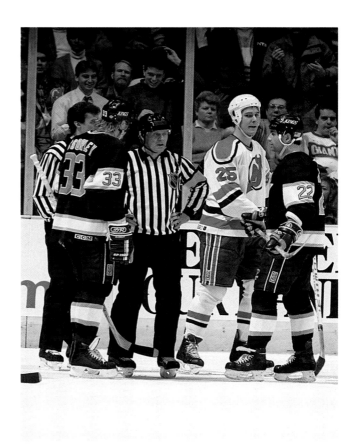

As the season progressed, Crowder's reputation preceded him.

team's toughness, the final ingredient for success in New Jersey.

A win over the Rangers, 3–2, capped a three-game winning streak, but the Devils had lost their only two games on the road. The following night at the Cap Centre, the Mr. Hyde version of the team made another appearance. In losing 4–0 to Washington, the Devils committed seven penalties in the third period, including an unsportsmanlike conduct call against Ken Daneyko, who argued with referee Bill McCreary over a questionable goal by Washington's John Druce.

"They got the momentum right away and played a well-disciplined game," asserted Cunniff, perhaps as a criticism of his team's tendency to take bad penalties. "They got those two quick goals and then shut us down pretty good." Terreri was again in the net, stopping 32 shots in the losing effort.

Three straight victories followed, over the lowly Islanders (8–1), the underachieving Sabres (5–1), and Pittsburgh (7–5), the latter being the most significant, extending New Jersey's home unbeaten streak to eight games. John MacLean, on his way to his third straight forty-goal season, scored his second goal. "I'll take the win," said Cunniff, "but it was a sloppy game. We're capable of playing much better and with more discipline," he added. "We got the team really high for the game. I was anxious myself and it feeds off, but it's up to me to know when it's too high."

Of course, over the next few games, nobody could accuse the Devils of being too high. A 6–3 loss to Calgary in the Saddledome continued the team's woes on the road, where they had beaten only the Islanders, who would finish last in the division.

Moreover, New Jersey was third in the league in penalty minutes with 377. "We keep talking about avoiding penalties and we keep doing it," fumed Cunniff, demonstrating the first signs of the frustration that would eventually contribute to his departure. He also benched Burke after the loss to the Flames, hoping to revive the team by inserting Terreri, along with seldom used Doug Brown and Pat Conacher.

It worked against the Islanders, who played the Devils tough this time and would have won except for Brown's two third-period goals which knotted the score at 5–5. "Brown gives us a spark," explained Cunniff; "he doesn't pace himself. He goes all out, gives you 100 percent all the time."

The same could not be said of the rest of the team. The Devils dropped six of eight games between October 30 and November 15, a significant date for the Devils. After losing his fourth straight game, 4–2 to Hartford, Sean Burke was booed loudly by the home fans. He responded angrily in the press. "I'm not playing for them—at least not for the ones who are booing," he said. "I'm playing for this team and the fans who stick with you, win or lose. The other ones can go to hell."

Nor would Burke repent later, insisting he meant what he said. "The thing is," he observed, "half the people at Byrne Arena are frustrated Ranger fans, frustrated from 1940," he added, noting the cheers that went through the arena at the sight of a winning Ranger score on the board.

It was a turning point for Burke, who saw little action at The Meadowlands—or anywhere else—after that. His record was 2–5–1 with a 4.24 goals against average. "We'll keep him away for a little while," said Cunniff, downplaying the incident.

In their next game against Philadelphia at The Meadowlands, Terreri came into his own, keying a brilliant 3–2 victory. Among his 27 saves was a stunning kick save of a penalty shot by Mike Ricci. "I think my

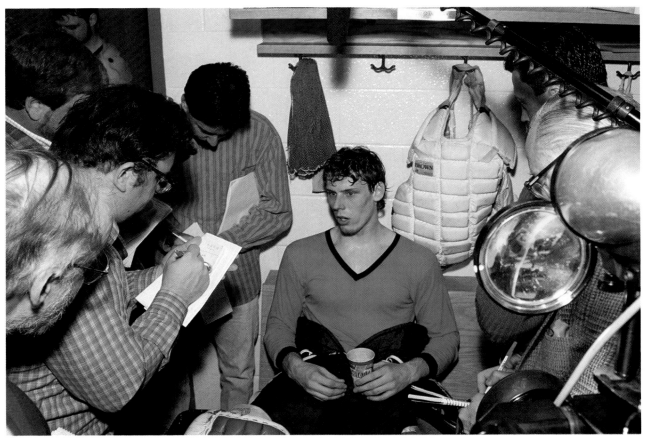

Sean Burke found that dealings with the media do not always flow smoothly.

quickness helps,'' said the diminutive goalie. ''It's a big asset and this is when it comes into play.''

MacLean had ten goals and Shanahan had five. But Fetisov was having a just average season, occasionally losing the puck and engaging in high-risk play. His partner, Kasatonov, was clearly the better of the two. Muller was slumping and would never reach top form, suffering his first truly disappointing season. He would finish with only 19 goals and 51 assists.

Throughout the next two months the inconsistent pattern continued. Terreri shined in goal, but otherwise the team was not as good in the standings as the roster Lamoriello had amassed. And Cunniff could not lift them to their potential. Occasionally, he would rip the team in his own quiet

way. ''He didn't rant or rave,'' noted Conacher, referring to a speech the coach had made during the November slump. ''He told us that if we practice like (bleep-bleeps), we'll play like (bleep-bleeps).'' The Devils beat Montreal the next night, 6–3.

But rarely did they ever climb higher than fourth in the standings, or win two games in a row, especially in January and February 1991. By January 15, rumors that Cunniff might be replaced began to surface. ''I haven't felt any pressure,'' he claimed, following a 6–1 loss to the Kings at The Meadowlands, the team's sixth loss in a row. ''I put a lot of pressure on myself,'' he added. ''It's a mental thing right now, but I'm not under the gun from the organization.''

But the Devils' lackluster play continued

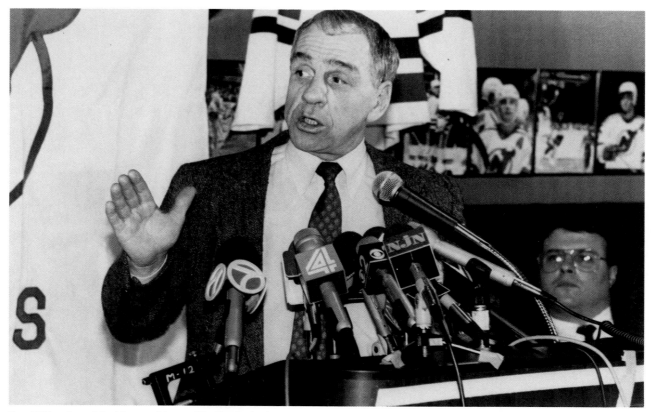

Tom McVie returned for his second tour at The Meadowlands.

through the end of February. Fetisov was upset about being benched for two games in mid-February, and that aggravated the situation. "I don't know how he got so out of sync like this," said Cunniff, who was answering more and more that way. "We can't afford to go any further like this."

After a typically lifeless Devils performance in a 3–1 loss to Boston, Cunniff criticized his team's desire. "They have no intensity, no will to win, and no character," he claimed, before storming out of his room, with parting words to his players: "I wish somebody would come in here so I could beat the crap out of them!"

The next day Cunniff was replaced by Utica coach Tom McVie.

"Making this type of decision is never easy," said Lamoriello. "The reasons for making the coaching change now are varied and numerous. At this stage of the season we feel our prospects remain very

strong and that Tom McVie is the man who can get the most out of our team in the stretch run."

McVie had been the Devils' second head coach in New Jersey. He coached the club for 60 games in the 1983-84 season after taking over for Billy MacMillan and guided the club to a 15–38–7 record. He had been serving in the organization for the past seven years as coach in Utica for the American Hockey League.

"I'm not here to make friends," McVie said. "The team has been up and down, one good game, followed by a bad one. It is the opinion of the organization that I'm the choice to handle the rest of the season and get New Jersey into the playoffs."

McVie would accomplish that task but the challenge, at times, seemed monumental. The battle for playoff berths was typically keen with only the Islanders apparently incapable of keeping up with the pack.

What would McVie do to put the Devils back on track?

"I believe in discipline and hard work, and I won't be afraid to go into the dressing room between periods and tell them if they are not working," he asserted.

McVie's debut as coach against the Islanders at Nassau Coliseum on March 5, 1991, a day after he was officially hired, was inauspicious. Al Arbour's skaters won 4–3 despite a pair of goals by John MacLean and another by Laurie Boschman, who continued to make the trade Lamoriello made for him look good.

The road swing continued with a 3–3 tie in Buffalo that offered hope mostly because of a come-from-behind effort sparked by Brendan Shanahan's goal just when it appeared another loss was going to be written in the standings. It was on to Winnipeg and yet another disheartening squeaker, and another 4–3 defeat.

Unlike Cunniff, McVie seemed better able to shake off the losses and maintain an energetically positive attitude. His buoyancy was catching and, despite, the torpor that characterized the club in Cunniff's final month, there now was an upbeat quality that inevitably would produce victories.

The turnabout occurred upon the Devils' return home on March 13. They edged Toronto 3–2 with Alexei Kasatonov scoring the game-winner and followed that with a resounding 5–2 bashing of the Rangers. Again Lamoriello's preseason trades paid off as Boschman checked fiercely and Claude Lemieux banged in two critical goals.

However, the euphoria of beating the Rangers may have caused a letdown the following night at Hartford, where the Whalers stunned the Devils 6–2. Could they get their act together again or would they falter as they had under Cunniff?

A major test would be provided by the Pittsburgh Penguins, who would visit The Meadowlands on March 19. If the Devils could take the measure of the future Stanley Cup champions, it would be a major psychological victory. And they did, to the tune of 5–4 with Patrik Sundstrom displaying some of his best hockey of the season. The slick Swede contributed two goals including the game-winner.

"The season had been frustrating for me," said Sundstrom. "It was a rollercoaster year for the whole team and my own game was the same way. Hopefully, we can straighten things out from here on."

It remained a neck-and-neck race between Philadelphia, Washington, Pittsburgh and the Devils. New Jersey wanted wins, but if ties can be like wins, they would take them anyway.

McVie showed his faith in Sean Burke, starting him on March 21 for what would be a three-game road trip including stops in Chicago, Montreal, and, finally, Madison Square Garden. This would be as challenging as any trio of contests could be since the Blackhawks were traditionally dominating at Chicago Stadium, the Canadiens invariably won at the Forum and, well, need we say anymore of the Rangers' home crowd.

Burke accepted, met his assignment head-on, and held the Hawks to two goals while Boschman and MacLean provided the Devils with enough for a much-needed point. MacLean's goal made it 2–2 when it appeared that game might belong to Chicago. The Devils now had a tenuous grip on third place but would drop to fourth the next day when Washington won. The Capitals had 76 to the Devils 75.

"We may not be winning consistently," said McVie, "but we're playing well and the tie against Chicago showed me a lot."

The hope now was that New Jersey could stay ahead of the faltering Flyers. A pair of 3–3 ties in Montreal and New York provided some relief until the club returned to Byrne on March 27 to play Hartford.

McVie remembered how the Whalers had been kill-joys less than two weeks earlier. He was determined to see that there was no repeat—but it was close.

Once again McVie started Burke after Terreri had played against the Rangers, and it was evident that Hartford would not play the pushover. It was also clear that if the Devils could somehow produce two points they would, for all intents and purposes, have a playoff berth clinched, although not mathematically.

Kirk Muller opened the scoring at 4:50 of the first period, beating Peter Sidorkiewicz in the Hartford net. Doug Brown gave the home crowd more reassurance at 12:08 with a rejuvenated Slava Fetisov providing a critical assist.

The Whalers were not about to cooperate with any premature celebrations. Former Devil Pat Verbeek sandwiched goals around one by Zarley Zalapski to give Hartford a 3–2 lead. Again, a rallying force was needed, and this time is was Brendan Shanahan coming through at 9:32 of the third period. From there to the end of regulation both goaltenders held fast, sending the critical match into overtime.

A tie wouldn't have been disastrous for McVie & Co., but the win still was more desirable at this juncture. The Devils had that in mind as the overtime approached the third minute when they charged the Hartford net forcing a scramble. Doug Brown captured the elusive rubber and tucked it home for the winner at 2:47.

One night later Washington blanked Philadelphia, 3–0, and the Devils had officially clinched a playoff berth. They would end their regular campaign with a record of 32 wins, 33 losses and 15 ties. Their 79 points put them three ahead of fifth-place Philadelphia, two behind third-place Wash-ington and six behind the second-place Rangers.

In retrospect, first place might even have been accomplished. New Jersey wound up nine behind Pittsburgh. Had the Devils been able to reverse the four losses to the last-place Islanders, two at the hands of sub-par Hartford, and embarrassing defeats to Minnesota, Quebec and Toronto, it would have been a lot different. But, as the sage has said, "there is much virtue in if."

But the Devils were in and that's what counted most. They would meet Patrick Division champion Pittsburgh and were confident of their chances.

"We're in a real good position," said Shanahan. "We're on the bottom looking up. We seem to play real well in that position."

Bruce Driver added, "We match up well with them. We have a lot of talent in this room. We realize the kind of hockey we have to play to beat Pittsburgh. We've started to play disciplined on the road."

Eric Weinrich, who had ripened in this his rookie year into a gifted defenseman, was not awed by Pittsburgh. "The keys to beating the Penguins," said Weinrich, "are not getting into a shootout with them and frustrating their top players. Mario Lemieux and Paul Coffey are dangerous anytime, but if we play a tight-checking game and don't give them a lot of shots, we can beat them."

There was, however, a harsh reality to face; the Devils had an 0–4 record at Pittsburgh's Civic Arena where the first two games of the series would be played.

The headline on Rich Chere's Newark *Star-Ledger* column was ominous: DEVILS' ODDS LONGER THAN THEY 'LOOK'.

None of the experts were certain which way McVie would go in terms of his starting goaltender, but he ended speculation by announcing that Chris Terreri would start.

Doug Brown scored shorthanded, then had one called back in Game Three.

"Both guys are totally ready to go," he said. "I sat and thought about it, and I guess I really don't know how or why I decided the way I did."

Terreri did not disappoint, nor did the Devils.

After Mario Lemieux gave Pittsburgh a 1–0 lead on a second period power play, Peter Stastny responded with a New Jersey power play goal. Stastny gave the Devils a 2–1 lead when he circled the net and scored at 4:12 of the third period. Fifty seconds later, Boschman increased the Devils' lead, beating goalie Tom Barrasso on a two-on-one rush with a shot high into the net.

Terreri took care of the rest of business, and the Devils tromped into the dressing room with a 3–1 win. "We tried to frustrate them," acknowledged Stastny. "If you're used to scoring goals and you don't score, it gets you. You doubt. You question."

McVie called it "old-fashioned hockey," and added, "I don't want fire-engine hockey. I don't believe in that. I'm really into checking. It was outstanding checking."

The possibility of going two-up on the road whetted the appetite of every New Jersey player. They were secure in the knowledge that they played well, got the goaltending and might even play better the second time around. They also understood that Pittsburgh would be ready in Game Two at home.

Nevertheless, McVie's foot soldiers attacked the Penguins with a passion. They went ahead 1–0, 2–1, and then came back from a 3–4 deficit to tie the game at four early in the third period, forcing overtime. They were outshooting and outworking Pittsburgh, and now all they needed was one goal against Barrasso to go home with a two-games-to-none lead.

Time and again New Jersey skaters penetrated the Penguins' defense but, always, Barrasso was a giant. He robbed Claude Lemieux, Doug Brown, and Bruce Driver of potential winners and then it was approaching the nine minute mark with the game still tied at four.

Until then Jaromir Jagr, the Penguins' skilled rookie, had not been particularly noticeable, but the big, bushy-haired 19-year-old suddenly made himself apparent. He started a powerful rush along the right boards, catching Devils defenseman Tommy Albelin out of position. John MacLean covered him and faced Jagr in a one-on-one situation in the right circle.

"I tried to stop him from getting to the net," said MacLean, "but he popped away."

Jagr skated to the front of the net, eluded defenseman Ken Daneyko and then flicked the puck at Terreri. "I got most of the shot," said the goalie, "but it hit me in the helmet and went in. It was a great play."

The time was 8:52 of the overtime. The score was 5–4 for Pittsburgh and the series tied at one. It was on to The Meadowlands. The Devils outplayed the Penguins in two straight but were deadlocked in the opening round.

Game Three was little different from the others — close! The Devils battled back three times, on a pair of power-play goals by Brendan Shanahan and a shorthanded goal by Doug Brown. With 1:22 left in the third period the crowd rose as one thinking Doug Brown had stuffed the winner past Tom Barrasso but referee Andy Van Hellemond ruled no goal.

"I made the pipe and put it across the goal line," said Brown. "I could see across the goal line, and it was six inches over. The goalie had his arm cocked in a V, and pulled it back."

No matter. The referee, right or wrong, had ruled against New Jersey. The Devils had to hope for a break their way. There was a break — right away, as a matter of fact — but it went the OTHER way.

McVie had all engines firing against Pittsburgh.

Having "lost" a goal, the Devils tried again forcing the Penguins into a desperation clearing attempt. Phil Bourque hoisted a Texas Leaguer toward the New Jersey net. Terreri figured that Weinrich would glove the puck and move it out of danger, but the defenseman was backskating and seemed to misjudge its trajectory by a few feet.

The rubber hit the ice before Weinrich could get his stick on it, and, lo and behold, there was Mark Recchi on top of the puck and—poof! just like that—it was in the net. There were only 50 seconds left when Pittsburgh got the winner.

Demoralizing would hardly be an adequate term to describe the incident. "It was a tough game to lose," said Terreri, "but it was just a bad break. It hit the ice and bounced up as I was starting out to get it."

Amazingly, the Devils were the better team in terms of the game's ebb and flow but were down two to one. Well, there was only one thing to do; pick themselves up, dust themselves off, and start all over again.

That done, everything was honky-dory. They hit the Penguins from the start of Game Four to the finish, and when all was said and done, New Jersey had a 4–1 edge. Claude Lemieux opened the scoring, followed by Stastny's deflection. A 2–0 lead lasted into the third period when Mario Lemieux scored on a five-on-three power play, but then MacLean and Claude Lemieux iced the game with less than three minutes remaining.

It was a mean game and, at one point, Coffey tried to outflank Fetisov along the right boards. Slava attempted a stick-to-stick check but his stick accidentally nicked Coffey above the left eye. The Penguin was taken to Newark's United Hospital for examination.

"I didn't mean to hurt him," Fetisov insisted. "It was an accident."

McVie enthused over the Devils' overall robust play and their relentless checking. "That's the way the game of hockey is meant to be played," he said. "A lot of guys were laying around the ice. Hey, this isn't a girls' game. If it was, we'd be wearing dresses."

In a calm moment McVie had to acknowledge what was rapidly becoming apparent. His skaters had outplayed first-place Pittsburgh in virtually every game. The series was now tied at two, heading back to the Civic Arena.

A quick burst in Period One of Game Five, and the Devils were ahead 2–0 on goals by MacLean and Bruce Driver. Terreri maintained the shutout until the start of the third period when the Penguins rallied for a pair before the four-minute mark. The crowd was into it, as they say, but the Devils were unruffled. They stayed with the Penguins, hoping for that all-important but often elusive opening.

They got it on a giveaway by Pittsburgh's Scott Young. Kirk Muller slid an ideal power-play right-to-left pass across the slot. Fetisov sped to the net where Claude Lemieux awaited developments. In a trice, the red light was on. It appeared to have hit Lemieux and then Fetisov swiped at it with his stick as it flew past Barrasso.

The Penguins launched a counter-offensive in an attempt to gain a draw before overtime, but Pat Conacher captured the puck and fed Doug Brown, who fired it into the empty net with 22 seconds remaining. The Devils had won, 4–2, and now led the series three games to two.

"We showed some great character coming back to win after they had tied it," said defenseman Lee Norwood. "That's what impresses me about this team."

Beat writers for both teams were impressed with the Devils' consistently superior play over the five games. This was no fluke; McVie had New Jersey doing the right things and now, as the series reverted to Byrne Arena for Game Six, an opening-round triumph was within the Devils' grasp.

The capacity crowd roared when the red, green, and white-shirted skaters took the ice. More than 19,000 spectators sensed that they were in for the kill, and there was every reason to believe so. With their top goalie Tom Barrasso sidelined, the Penguins inserted back-up Frank Pietrangelo in the net. Coffey, still recuperating from his eye injury, also was *hors de combat*.

Then, three things happened that would forever alter the flow of the series that had been in New Jersey's direction. The Devils, after an early goal, somehow lost their momentum. Mario Lemieux and Kevin Stevens took over, and the Devils found themselves trailing 4–1 in the second period.

It was then that the third—and most trying—episode unfolded. Having fought back on goals from Weinrich and Claude Lemieux, the Devils poured volley after volley at Pietrangelo. Just past the 18:25 point in the second period, Claude Lemieux fed Boschman who was moving directly at the Penguins' goalie.

As video replay after video replay later confirmed, the puck moved LEGALLY from Boschman's skate to his stick and thence into the net. An eruption of collective joy cascaded down from the upper reaches of the arena as the red light flashed. But just as quickly, the roar subsided.

Why? That was what everyone wondered.

Referee Bill McCreary was waving his arms in the unmistakable "No Goal!" manner. McCreary refused to consult with his linesmen or, for that matter, anyone. It was an arbitrary, split second decision that just happened to be wrong. And since the NHL was not employing video replay as an aide in such circumstances at the time, there was little the Devils could do but argue; and

then get on with the game.

Oh yes, they had plenty of opportunities to tie the match in the third period, but a combination of ill luck and Pietrangelo got in the way, and when the final buzzer sounded, it was still 4–3 Pittsburgh.

And what might have happened had Boschman's tally counted? All signs suggest that the Devils were ready to take the game away from Pittsburgh. "Who knows how the game would have gone without that bad call," said Brendan Shanahan with what seemed to be as sensible an answer as any.

"We didn't get back to the basics until it got to be 4–1," said McVie.

Well, the Devils would have one more chance to do so, although to a man they did not want to return to Pittsburgh under any circumstances. Now, they had no choice. "We've overcome a lot in this series," said Driver. "Now we only have to win one more game."

It was not to be; not from the very onset of Game Seven. With Coffey back in the lineup, the Penguins appeared revitalized overnight. They came at the Devils from the opening face-off and finally beat Terreri at 6:17 of the first period when Jiri Hrdina captured his own rebound and fired a close-in drive past Chris. Mario Lemieux followed with a power-play score to give Pittsburgh a 2–0 edge at the end of the first.

Perhaps the Devils might have recouped their losses with a vibrant second period, but the little-used Hrdina scored before the period was a minute old, and now the Devils were down by three. From that point on, the Penguins threw a defensive blanket in front of Pietrangelo and ran out the clock. It was 4–0 at the end, and New Jersey's skaters sat slumped in the dressing room with only thoughts of what might have been.

"We could have won the series in the sixth game," said Driver. "We should have

Boschman celebrates disallowed goal which would have tied Game Six.

won it in the seventh game, but the bottom line is that we lost."

John MacLean was more succinct. "It's very disappointing."

As it happened, the Penguins moved into the second round, beat Washington, and then successively ousted Boston and Minnesota to annex the Stanley Cup. The victors said New Jersey was the best team they had faced in the entire playoffs.

Who knows what might have been had the Devils — the better team in five of seven playoff games — won Game Six. Would they have taken the Caps, Bruins, and North Stars? We'll never know.

What we do know is that Lamoriello immediately got down to the business of improving his team for 1991-92. He began by re-signing Tom McVie to a new coaching contract, after which he hired Robbie Ftorek as assistant coach. That done, 1980 Gold Medal hero Herb Brooks was named coach of the Utica Devils of the American League.

It was the start of a re-shaping process to mold the Devils into big winners for the rest of the 1990s.

17

A PAIR OF COMEBACK KIDS

Over the years, the Devils have developed a number of outstanding draft choices. Ranking at the top of the list is Kirk Muller, who was selected first by the team (second overall) in 1984 and epitomized the work ethic that became the club's imprimatur. To say that Muller emerged as Mister Devil would hardly be an exaggeration.

He made an immediate impact on the franchise and to this day remains one of the most affable spokesmen any athletic organization could desire. If Muller suffered from any "problem," it was the fact that he was selected immediately after Mario Lemieux in the 1984 draft and inevitably was compared to the big, gifted Penguin for years since then.

Muller had nothing to apologize about. He was an instant asset and matured as a rookie. His point total (54) was impressive as a rookie and grew steadily for the next three seasons. In that sense, one can say he fulfilled many of his early notices. Muller, it

can be said, never was counted out.

However, there were two New Jersey draft choices who were virtually dismissed as failures, yet managed to lift themselves off the ice and emerge as major cogs in the Devils' machine. John MacLean was viewed as a high draft pick who turned out to be a bust while Chris Terreri appeared to be a collegiate whiz-kid who was too small to make it in the bigs. At best, it was felt, Terreri would be considered a "decent backup goalie." That is, if he was lucky.

Had the Devils' management—Lou Lamoriello in particular—not been sensitive to their needs and patient to a fault, heaven knows what path their respective NHL graphs would have taken. Conceivably, either or both would have been traded or dispatched to the minors, spirit broken, career gone to pot.

Fortunately, the MacLean-Terreri storylines turned to the happy side. Each can echo the words of William Shakespeare—

"Sweet are the uses of adversity" — and say that he benefitted from the hard times and came out all the better for it.

In any case, the two have been singled out, not because they were better than others or that teammates did not deserve special treatment, but rather because Johnny Mac and Scary symbolize the twelve-year Devils saga of rebounding from adversity.

• • •

There were several hints that Chris Terreri could give New Jersey the brand of goaltending security that any contending club requires, but they seemed vague and fragile on the night of October 5, 1989.

Until that time, Sean Burke was the undisputed number one netminder in East Rutherford, and if you didn't believe it, ask any hockey writer between Winnipeg and Washington.

If any NHL fact was etched in stone — other than Wayne Gretzky was the best center on the Los Angeles Kings — it had to be Burke's mortgage on the rectangular acreage in front of the pipes.

How could it be otherwise?

"What Sean did for us in the spring of '88 put him front-and-center as far as goaltending was concerned," said defenseman Craig Wolanin, who skated that miracle mile. "Everybody figured he'd be our main man for a long time."

But the fates have a way of developing opportunities when least expected. A pre-training camp injury had shelved Burke, and Terreri was designated by coach Jim Schoenfeld to open the 1989-90 campaign at Philadelphia's Spectrum.

In this less than comfortable environment, Terreri would have an opportunity to state his case, and he did it spades. Yes, he could handle pressure. Yes, the little guy could come up big against the behemoths, and, yes, he deserved to be considered top

banana.

"What I'm striving for," said the Providence native, "is consistency. When I play well, I play very well. But sometimes it's not there. It'll get better in time."

Since Burke's return virtually assured Terreri a place on the bench, there was some question whether Chris could ever hone his game to the level of sharpness he desired. Sure enough, when Burke healed, it was status quo ante; Sean WAS number one and that was that.

Or was it?

Slowly but relentlessly, Terreri produced memorable moments in 1989-90; like the night he starred in a 38-save game in Winnipeg, assuring New Jersey a win over the Jets that they had absolutely no business taking.

"It's vital for a guy like Chris to come in and play like that," Burke acknowledged. "On this team we have to have a second goalie who can go in and win games. Bob Sauve did it the year we went to the playoffs."

Ah, but the stigma of "second goalie" was one that not-so-tacitly suggested a caste system when performance dictated a more equitable balance. Coach John Cunniff, who replaced Jim Schoenfeld early in the campaign, acknowledged Terreri's skill while more wins fortified Chris' case.

Noteworthy was a Saturday afternoon match on February 24, 1990, against the powerful Chicago Blackhawks. This is a club Terreri earlier had beaten with 37 saves in October. In this second encounter of the close kind, teammates had so abandoned the neatly-packaged netminder that Frank Brown of the *Daily News* said, "the Devils played well enough to get their butts blown out of most NHL rinks."

That they didn't on this winter afternoon was because Terreri handled the four-by-six-foot airspace behind him as if by radar-

foot airspace behind him as if by radar-control. He made 46 saves, allowed two goals, while his mates scraped together three for the win.

"We know that any other night Chicago would have won," said Cunniff. "We lost games when we played much better, but this one belonged to Chris."

And maybe, just maybe, the thinking was swinging to a point where number-one goalie could, someday, be Terreri, not Burke. It still sounded like sacrilege to some, but look at the record. Down the final March chute it was Terreri who led the Devils out of a late-season slump and into second place, taking eight out of the Devils' final twelve wins.

Was that enough to persuade Cunniff to start Chris in the playoff opener against Washington? Heck, no. The Burke mystique prevailed and Terreri was back at the end of the bench in Game One at Byrne Arena.

The result was not what the coach had anticipated. Burke allowed some questionable goals and made an errant pass that led to Dino Ciccarelli's rebound goal at 5:34 of overtime in Washington's 5–4 victory.

That did it.

Terreri took over for Game Two—and won. He returned for Game Three and won that game as well, although his teammates supported him with a popgun offense.

Cunniff gambled and returned with Burke in Game Four. In the view of some strategists, the coach could afford a "throwaway game" since he had the two-games-to-one lead, and, perhaps, Burke would come up big.

He didn't. The winning groove was disrupted, and the Devils, with Terreri back in the pipes, would lose the next two and the series. If anything was learned from the experience, it simply was that Chris Terreri, whatever his physical dimensions, had lifted his game to Burke's level and perhaps beyond.

The point was reiterated time and again during the 1990-91 season during which Terreri posted 24 wins, 21 losses, and seven ties compared with Burke's 8–12–8. As for goals against average, it was Terreri on top, 2.91 to 3.59.

What needed to be added; the numbers said it all.

After a patient struggle, Chris had become *numero uno*.

• • •

Each decade in the National Hockey League, a skater is bred who stands removed from his peers, not because of style or speed, but rather that tangible intangible known as "clutchability."

In the 1930s it was a Boston Bruin named Mel Hill who scored so many over-time playoff goals he eventually was nick-named Sudden Death.

In the 1940s and 1950s Maurice (The Rocket) Richard of the Montreal Canadiens knocked in the NHL's version of the Grand Slam so often, he was nicknamed the Babe Ruth of Hockey.

And so it went. More recently, Bob Nystrom did it for the Islanders at a time when New Jersey's new organization was hunting for junior-level players who some-day would manufacture the big ones in the big moments. A month after Nystrom had played on his fourth straight Stanley Cup winner, the Devils wrestled with the question: who to pick in the 1983 draft. They picked sixth overall and opted for a smiling broth of a boy who lived in Oshawa, Ontario, and played three seasons with the Junior Generals in his hometown.

This was not what you would call an automatic winner.

There must have been many a night when Devils scouts agonized over the choice. MacLean played 23 games for New Jersey in 1983-84 and scored a grand total of one goal! Not even an assist. He was shipped back to Oshawa to get more work and returned to The Meadowlands a year later for who-knew-what.

The "guaranteed" label had been removed. No warranties existed for John MacLean. Just hope that time would burnish the rough edges and the glitter that the scouts had projected would finally become apparent at The Meadowlands. In 1984-85 he was given a full run in the bigs and responded with a modest 13–20–33 and 44 penalty minutes in 61 games.

"The confidence was not there yet," the Smiling One would explain.

Nobody rushed him. A year later he made it through 74 games and lifted his numbers to 21–36–57. Not bad. In 1986-87 it was even better: a full 80 games, good for 31–36–67.

"By that time," he explained, "the confidence had come. I began realizing that I could play in this league. And I wanted to prove to the organization that they didn't make a mistake picking me."

There were, however, mistakes in the manner that MacLean was managed. He didn't respond to Doug Carpenter's harsh handling and slumped until Jim Schoenfeld moved behind the bench.

The rest is delicious Devils history. MacLean's pantheon of puck heroics are well-chronicled elsewhere.

Suffice to say, he put New Jersey on the playoff map with his overtime goal against the Blackhawks on the final night of 1987-88. He continued to orchestrate awesome vignettes, sending two playoff games against the Islanders into overtime with dramatic goals in the final two minutes of regulation time.

Enough? No sir and madam. MacLean wrote the requiem for the outgoing Washington Capitals in the seventh game with the third-period game-winner. And when the Devils required resuscitation in Game Six of the Wales Conference finals, Johnny Mac scored the tie-breaker late in the second period, leading the Devils to a 6–3 victory.

Was it a fluke?

Please.

A year later MacLean turned in a career-best season with 42–45–87 in 74 games. If you will excuse the bromide, he had remained New Jersey's Johnny-On-The-Spot through 1990-91 when he reached the 45-goal plateau.

If ever a case could be made for patience and fortitude, John MacLean had made it.

18

1991-92:
A YEAR OF RECORDS

Having taken the eventual Stanley Cup champion Pittsburgh Penguins to a seventh and final game in their 1991 playoff, the Devils entered the off-season secure in the knowledge that they had performed better than any other club against the ultimate world-beaters.

While this was a notable accomplishment, president and general manager Lou Lamoriello realized that there still was more to add to the plate. There also were unexpected events that would emerge, forcing adjustments to the lineup and eventually setting the stage for a dynamic 1991-92 season.

The first and most telling event of the summer occurred in June when winger Brendan Shanahan, a Type 1 free agent, signed with the St. Louis Blues. As a result of Shanahan's move, the Devils were entitled to compensation, and Lamoriello in a move which some viewed as a gamble, designated Scott Stevens as his choice.

An imposing (6-2, 210 pounds) defenseman, the 27-year-old Stevens was well-known to the Devils' fans, having previously starred for the Washington Capitals. The hard-hitting backliner had been a free agent pick-up by the Blues from Washington a year earlier and that cost St. Louis five first-round picks over five years.

Blues general manager Ron Caron countered with an offer of forward Rod Brind'Amour and goalie Curtis Joseph. The decision, which would be made by veteran NHL arbitrator Judge Edward J. Houston, aroused considerable interest throughout the league. Meanwhile, the judge met in Toronto with representatives from both teams and heard their arguments.

"We're going to the judgment with the confidence that our offer is the most fair," said Caron. "We're ready to pay what we owe."

Judge Houston determined that the Blues owed Stevens and thus, in September

Scott Stevens arrived and immediately reshaped the Devils' defense.

1991, Scott became a Devil. This was a clear-cut victory for Lamoriello but hardly his only off-season triumph. Less obtrusively, Troy Crowder also went the free agent route and signed with the Detroit Red Wings. The Devils were awarded forwards Randy McKay and Dave Barr, each of whom would have significantly better seasons than Crowder.

Changes also were being made to fortify the general staff. Lamoriello hired two American hockey legends, Herb Brooks and Robbie Ftorek, and placed them in key positions. The 1980 United States Olympic hero, Brooks was named coach of the Devils' American League farm team in Utica.

"We want Herb to develop our young players in Utica," said Lamoriello. "We want the best-qualified coaches we can get. That's why we hired Herb and Robbie."

Ftorek was named assistant coach to New Jersey head coach Tom McVie. "Herb Brooks is a good coach," said McVie, "and I know Robbie Ftorek is a good hockey man. We've got a great coaching staff here. It's great for the Devils."

Training camp was exciting, if nothing else, for McVie, Ftorek and Brooks, to say the least because the re-shaping of the hockey club still was taking place. On September 20, Lamoriello delivered another blockbuster move when he traded captain Kirk Muller and goalie Roland Melanson to the Montreal Canadiens for Stephane Richer and Tom Chorske, both forwards.

This was a particularly meaningful move for New Jersey because Muller had been a major part of the club's fabric for so long. But he also had been conspicuous by his

Acquired in a blockbuster deal, Stephane Richer added 50-goal potential to the roster.

Craig Billington saw years of patience pay off when he arrived on the NHL scene to stay.

"We traded for an explosive talent in Richer," said Lamoriello. "He gives our club a dimension it needed. He can shoot the puck."

"I don't mind pressure," said Richer. "You have to deal with it with this job."

Claude Lemieux, who had teamed with Richer in Montreal, endorsed the move. "The pressure isn't going to bother him," said Lemieux. "He'll just play better and better if you put that kind of pressure on him."

As training camp unfolded, it became evident that the Devils had amassed one of the most formidable defense units in the league and certainly the best in the club's history. Stevens was teamed with Eric Weinrich, who was fast developing into a confident multi-purpose rearguard. The Russians, Slava Fetisov and Alexei Kasatonov, returned more acclimatized to North American-style hockey than ever. Then there were veteran Devils Bruce Driver and Ken Daneyko along with top utility defender Tommy Albelin.

"We'll be one of the best defensive clubs in the league," Fetisov opined.

Driver: "Stevens is a much-needed piece to the puzzle for our team. The biggest plus for us in getting a player like that is his physical game."

The departure of Muller meant it was time to name a new captain, and Driver got the nod. Slowly and painstakingly, the Devils began to take form as training camp unfolded. On September 30, they played an exhibition game at Byrne Meadowlands Arena against the New York Islanders. The seemingly unimportant evening turned out to be a telling one for New Jersey.

Less than six minutes into the game a melee erupted in the corner to the left of the Islanders' goal. MacLean wound up on the bottom of a heap of players and emerged with damage to the medial collat-

absence in the playoffs, and while there was no questioning his work ethic, Muller disappointed in the points department. The feeling was that a 50-goal man such as Richer would provide more tangible production for the New Jersey offense. What few realized at the time was the hidden gem Lamoriello had unearthed in Chorske.

eral ligamant of his right knee. Although it was unknown at the time, MacLean would be lost for the entire season. On the plus side was a 9-1 romp over the Islanders and the emergence of top draft choice Scott Niedermayer as a prize prospect.

It has long been Devils policy not to use injuries as an alibi, and so they went about the business of compensating for the loss of MacLean. By opening night, October 5, 1991, the Devils were ready to launch their new season. Their opponent, ironically enough, would be the St. Louis Blues, led by Brendan Shanahan and Brett Hull.

In many ways it was a memorable event for the 15,258 fans, not to mention the new Devils. "I was very nervous before the game," Richer admitted. The same could be said for newcomers Tom Chorske and Scott Stevens.

But if the trio did have butterflies, they weren't apparent to the enthusiastic crowd. Less than a minute after the opening face-off the new Devils went about the business of proving they were at home in New Jersey.

Richer took a pass from Chorske, spun like a top in the left circle and then powered a shot through a maze of players, beating goalie Vincent Riendeau. The time was 49 seconds and the Devils were off and running for the new season.

To underline his point that he enjoyed his switch to New Jersey, Richer replied with his second goal less than ten minutes later. While captain Bruce Driver sat out an interference penalty, Richer combined with Slava Fetisov on a two-on-one break against defenseman Mario Marois. The Russian ace orchestrated the play by patiently retaining the puck until Richer reached the slot. Slava then skimmed a synchronized pass which Stephane directed home for his 200th NHL goal.

As if to prove that he shouldn't be the forgotten man in the Richer deal, Chorske demonstrated his multiple skills after the Blues had reduced the margin to 2-1 late in the second period. With the Devils skating shorthanded, Tom displayed his immense forechecking skills and pushed the Blues into a costly turnover. The Devils' Doug Brown retrieved the puck, delivered the biscuit to Chorske who sent a 50-footer past Riendeau on the glove side at 15:14. That not only was the backbreaker but also turned out to be the game-winner. The Devils added to their 3-1 margin and emerged with a 7-2 victory.

The juxtaposition of Stevens vs. Shanahan was striking throughout the contest. Though Brendan scored a goal, he was roundly booed throughout. The fans sided with Stevens who played a robust game on the blue line.

Among the happiest players were Richer and Chorske. "I couldn't have hoped that it would go better," said Chorske. "That's about as well as things have gone for me in a long time. I've gotten confidence and I feel appreciated in New Jersey."

Richer: "It's just great the way the night turned out."

While Richer fortified the offense, the Devils were getting solid work in goal where Chris Terreri was demonstrating that, yes, he was worthy of the number one slot. Terreri had played so capably in the 1991 playoffs that coach Tom McVie gave him the nod over the incumbent Sean Burke.

Displeased over the state of affairs, Burke opted to play for Team Canada rather than New Jersey. It was a critical move and earned criticism for Sean from segments of the media. "Burke has made a mess of things for himself since Terreri became the number one goalie by outplaying Burke," wrote Hugh Delano in *The New York Post*.

With Burke absent, McVie replaced him with Craig Billington, and Biller, as he is affectionately known to his teammates,

For Bruce Driver, a combination of experience and poise led to the captaincy.

proved the ideal back to Terreri. He accepted his position without complaint and kept himself in mint condition, awaiting the call to serve.

Another player carefully watched was Driver, who replaced Muller as captain. In seven seasons, he had become "the best defenseman in Devils history," in the words of the Bergen Record's John Dellapina. He held records for goals (50), assists (205) and points (255) by a defenseman as the 1991-92 season began.

"Being named captain is definitely an opportunity for me to be recognized," said Driver. "I feel grateful for that and I feel I can do the job. I may be more of a quiet leader than anything. I'll try to lead by example but I realize I'll have to be more vocal in the locker room too."

The Devils followed their opening night triumph with a 4-2 win over the Chicago Blackhawks and a 6-5 edge over the Quebec Nordiques. Peter Stastny and Richer were leading the team in scoring, Terreri was sharp in goal and the defense, anchored by Stevens, bordered on airtight. There remained unanswered questions; namely, could the offense be maintained minus MacLean; would the Devils develop a killer instinct, and would Terreri perform capably long-term in Burke's absence.

Some positive answers came on October 26 when the brand-new San Jose Sharks invaded the Meadowlands. As for killer instinct, the Devils scored nine goals; as for Terreri, he posted his second career shutout and first of the season; as for the ailing MacLean, yes he was missed but enough of the healthy forwards were contributing in his absence to soften the blow.

One of them was Claude Lemieux. Night by night, the ebullient French-Canadian was evolving into one of Lamoriello's prime acquisitions. He had learned to control his volatile temper and was producing pivotal goals with regularity. Typical was the game-winner against San Jose. Stevens had fired a scorcher at goalie Jeff Hackett, but a rebound squirted loose and Lemieux shot it home with a rarely-used backhand shot.

Other positive signs manifested themselves as the calendar turned to November. McKay and Barr, who had been uncertain quantities, each put his personal stamp on the club. Extraordinarily focused, McKay became the quintessential checking forward who also scored the timely goal. Utterly fearless, Randy also was not averse to handling his dukes — he went toe-to-toe with the Sharks' enforcer Link Gaetz at Byrne Arena — although McKay almost never was one to foolishly instigate a fight.

"It's great to be getting a regular turn," said McKay. "I'll play tough and, if the occasion demands it, I'll scrap."

The veteran Barr, who had been injured in training camp, returned in late October and gradually worked his way into the lineup. His insights into the game and opportune use of the body made him a valuable member of the roster.

The same could be said for Billington, who made his first start with the club on October 31 at Calgary and responded with a 5-2 win. If nothing else, it signalled to McVie that Biller always would be ready when summoned to the net, a fact that would be reiterated throughout the campaign.

In beating the Flames, Billington stopped 34 of 36 shots and handed Calgary its first loss of the season. "I have a lot of pride in the role I play on this team," said Billington. "Whether I play one game or ten or twenty, that doesn't alter the pride I spoke about. I'm a goaltender. I'm doing what I love to do — play goal. I've been in the organization eight years. It hasn't been smooth sailing by any means. But now I'm here, in the NHL. That means a lot to me."

Bill Guerin provided a glimpse of the future with his '92 playoff performance.

It meant a lot to Richer when he finally faced his former teammates on the Montreal Canadiens. This was on November 8, 1991 at Byrne. The Habs came to Jersey riding the crest of a nine-game winning steak and a crowd of 13,507 was on hand for the match. Bothered by a groin strain that had caused him to miss three games a week earlier, Richer insisted on playing after the pregame warmup.

The Devils appreciated the decision, even more so after the game was tied 1-1 in the second period. Skating on a line with rookie center Kevin Todd and Chorske, Richer took Tom's pass — with Guy Carbonneau covering him like a tarpaulin — and beat Patrick Roy. Stephane scored the game-winner early in the third period after Todd stole the rubber at center ice. Kevin slid a pass to Richer on left wing and, though Roy was hugging the near post, the former Canadien stuffed the puck between the goalie's pads for the third and clinching goal in the 3-2 win.

"It was a big win," said a smiling Richer. "And to beat my best friend on the ice, Patrick Roy, twice. It was a wierd feeling when I scored the second goal because Patrick doesn't give up many like that. After playing Montreal, I really feel like a Devil now. I'm glad to be here."

Richer exhibited his scoring prowess through the autumn. On November 20 he produced a three-goal hat trick against the Washington Capitals at Byrne. The final goal came at 1:41 of sudden-death overtime after Alexei Kasatonov collected a rebound of a Richer shot and sent it to the goalmouth. Richer jumped on the loose puck and backhanded it past the sprawled Don Beaupre.

The win over Washington carried with it meaningful overtones. By mid-season the Patrick Division had unequivocally been rated the strongest in the NHL, and even the relatively weaker clubs like the Islanders and Flyers had proven they could more than hold their own against their divisional cousins.

While the Devils had established keen rivalries within the Patrick, there was no doubt that the sharpest of them all existed between New Jersey and the cross-Hudson New York Rangers. Even newcomers to the scene were quick to pick up on it. "When we play the Rangers," said Richer, "I feel the same way I felt when I was with Montreal and we played the Bruins. Every game was the Stanley Cup final. You had to win every time. They're the games where you see what kind of player you are. Every shift is important. The intensity level is high and you know you can blow a game with one mistake."

Doug Brown: "Whether you're underdogs on paper doesn't matter."

The Patrick wasn't the only rivalry in which the Devils were immersed. The success of ex-Canadiens Lemieux, Richer and Chorske stimulated considerable discussion amid the Montreal media, many of whom believed that coach Pat Burns had erred in his treatment of the trio, especially Lemieux and Richer. One such columnist, Rejean Tremblay of the influential daily *La Presse,* hammered away at the theme to a point where Burns felt obliged to belittle Lemieux and Richer.

"I'm not going to comment on that," replied Lemieux, who took an uncharacteristically subdued attitude toward Burns. "But I'm not surprised. It gives you an idea of why we didn't get along."

The New Jersey-Montreal rivalry was enhanced in yet another way; this time by a native Montrealer who now wore the Devils' colors. On January 29, 1992, Randy McKay impressed the Forum faithful to no end — not to mention many members of the McKay clan — with the most arresting performance of his still young big-league career.

Having won two straight on the road, the Devils managed to hold Montreal to a 3-3 tie well into the third period. At the nine minute mark, McKay accepted an Eric Weinrich pass, skated behind the Canadiens net and deceived the home defense into thinking he was attempting a pass. Instead, Randy drove around to the front of the net and wrapped the puck inside the left post.

"I kept going behind the net," said McKay, "and saw a commotion. That's when I snuck it through. I went hard to the net which is what the coaches want me to do."

It was McKay's second of two goals scored in front of his father, Hugh, several uncles and two cousins from Toronto. "For me it was a dream come true," McKay added. "I always wanted to be one of the 'Three Stars' but I never thought I'd ever be named the first star."

Lamoriello continued to retool his team as it headed toward the homestretch. In January he traded slumping 28-year-old veteran David Maley to Edmonton for 21-year-old former Ranger Troy Mallette. "We lacked a certain ingredient on the left side of the ice," said Lamoriello of the trade. "Troy gives us youth, aggressiveness, intimidation."

Coincidence or otherwise, Mallette's arrival coincided with a stirring mid-winter drive. Over a span of 18 games, New Jersey won 13, tied one and lost but four games. Where once they trailed the division-leading Rangers by 13 points, they had reduced the margin to 10 and hosted the Broadway Blueshirts on February 16, 1992, at the Meadowlands.

Every season there always are games that because of their intensity, artistry and overall quality set them apart from the norm; and this collision of the trans-Hudson rivals was a perfect example. "If you don't like a hockey game like this," said Tom McVie, "you ought to be covering tennis."

What the Devils did was cover Mark Messier — with Claude Lemieux. "He was with me everywhere on the ice," the Rangers' captain admitted. "When I went to the bench he almost sat down with me."

With Messier in check, the Devils chewed away at the Rangers' defense, building a 3-0 lead early in the third period. Undaunted, the Rangers replied with a pair of goals and came perilously close to tying the count until Lemieux relieved the pressure with an open-netter with 17 seconds remaining.

"Can you imagine seven games like that?" McVie told reporters after the game. "It could happen."

Seven playoff games in April between the Devils and Rangers had never happened before. The prospects of it happening in 1992 had never been more appealing now that the Devils had demonstrated that they could take the Rangers. New Jersey had now gone 14-4-1 in their last 19 games and had reduced the Rangers lead to but eight points.

One by one, Devils were coming to the fore. Lemieux was having a career season on the attack. Terreri was never better in goal and an assortment of defensemen were kicking their game up a notch. One in particular was Fetisov. The onetime Red Army ace had acclimatized himself to NHL play, combining cerebral strategic play with synchronized hitting. On February 18, Slava delivered the goods at a most opportune time.

Revitalized by a coaching change, the Flyers were making a determined bid for a playoff berth. It was important for the Devils to torpedo the Philadelphias before they became a major threat, particularly since the visitors tied the game at 3-3 with only five seconds remaining.

Having sent the match into overtime, the Flyers pressed for the killer but Barr corralled the rubber and moved it to Fetisov who was patrolling the left side of the Philadelphia zone. Slava moved to the left face-off circle and sized up the enemy positions. "My first thought was to shoot the puck low because (goalie) Ron Hextall is a big guy," said Fetisov. "Then I saw at the last moment he was coming out and the two top corners were open."

Fetisov's drive found the short side at 1:42 of the overtime and confirmed a suspicion the Russian had harbored all day. "I felt all day that I had to score," Slava allowed in the dressing room. "I've had a sore ankle and every game I get hit with the puck in the ankle. My luck had to change."

Unfortunately, the Devils luck was about to change — for the worse. Just when it appeared that the Jerseyites were going to take dead aim at first place, a succession of critical injuries detoured their climb to the top. During a stirring 4-4 comeback tie with the Blackhawks at Chicago Stadium, the Devils lost Stevens with a knee injury. Only a game later Barr was gone for the season with a grave hand injury at Winnipeg after Thomas Steen's skate sliced through his right wrist.

Disturbing though the injuries may have been, they did not send the Devils into panic. Rather, the club regrouped and continued to amaze. They had gone ten games (0-7-3) without a win at Madison Square Garden but on March 4 crafted a 5-4 win on one of the strangest plays of the entire season.

It began when Doug Brown flipped the puck into the Rangers' zone with fleet Tom Chorske in pursuit. Rangers defenseman Brian Leetch pursued Chorske whereupon goalie Mike Richter decided to vacate his net and intercept the disk. Realizing that Richter was a split-second late, Leetch

executed a driving pokecheck but only managed to slam into Richter.

Hunks of hockey players scattered in front of the New York net as if an earthquake had erupted. Meanwhile, rookie Jarrod Skalde who was following the play zeroed in on the skittering puck and illuminated the first goal of his NHL career as defenseman Jeff Beukeboom futilely dove to protect the empty net. Skalde's score gave the Devils a 5-4 victory.

"This was important to us," said defenseman Driver. "We have a chance to play this team in the playoffs."

Injuries continued to dog the Devils through the final month of the schedule but, by far, the most debilitating, roster-wise, was the loss of goalie Billington in a 2-2 tie with the Oilers at Northlands Coliseum. Edmonton forward Anatoli Semenov fell into Biller, sending him crashing into the net with 7:13 left in the second period. Although Craig attempted to continue the game, it soon became obvious that his maneuverability was gone. Terreri took over late in the period and finished the game. As bad luck would have it, Billington would be lost for the remainder of the regular season and the playoffs. This was followed by an enforced Terreri sabbatical when his back refused to cooperate and still the Devils hung in there.

Perhaps the most inspiring Devils win of the campaign took place during this agonizing run of wounds. On March 26, McVie was compelled to insert seven rookies into the lineup, including junior-age goaltender Martin Brodeur. Performing in his first major league game, Brodeur was the picture of calm as his mates skated him to a 3-0 lead. And when the home forces began wilting, the brush-cut Brodeur stood tall. His most memorable stop was posted after Adam Oates found Vladimir Ruzicka alone in front of the New Jersey net. The sharp-

Randy McKay displayed well-rounded skills which made him a lineup fixture.

shooting Bruin appeared to have a certain goal but Brodeur deflected the forehand shot with his arm, enabling the Devils to preserve a 4-2 edge.

Nobody knew it at the time, but that was to be the Devils last game for more than anyone had bargained for because of an unprecedented ten-day players' strike. As distasteful as the walkout was to all concerned, it did provide some unexpected solace. The interlude not only allowed the wounded to obtain some extra days to heal but also gave the high command time to evaluate some of the newcomers who would play a key role in upcoming playoff games. One of them was U.S. Olympic aspirant Bill Guerin, the Devils' first choice (fifth overall) in the 1989 entry draft.

The burly Guerin had scored 12 points (eight goals, four assists) in ten AHL games with Utica, including points in seven straight games. After Claude Lemieux suffered a bruised left ankle, Guerin was promoted to the big team and immediately impressed the general staff with his vitality. "Bill was the best right wing at Utica," Lamoriello explained.

When owners and the NHL Players' Association finally settled, the Devils resumed play at home against Washington on April 12. Lemieux summed up prevailing opinion when he asserted, "What matters to me is to be playing hockey!"

The Devils finished the season in fourth place with a 38-31-11 mark, the best in franchise history. In many ways it was a record-breaking season. Among the many club standards set were the following:
- Most points (87)
- Most wins at home (24)
- Longest winning streak (6 games)
- Fewest goals allowed (259)

The achievements meant a lot to both players and management, but there still was an important bit of business to handle.

After ten years of waiting, the Devils finally got their shot at the Rangers in the playoffs. As longtime New Jersey fan Yogi Berra so aptly put it, "This series will show what our guys are made of because the Rangers (first-place finishers overall) wound up on top."

A headline in the April 19 Sunday *Star Ledger* summed up prevailing strategic opinion on the series: STOPPING MESSIER DEVILS' NO. 1 PRIORITY.

It was no secret that the Devils had to contain the Rangers' captain and eventual Hart (MVP) Trophy-winner. Nor was it any mystery that New Jersey was an underdog against the Patrick Division leaders. Some experts went as far as to pick New York in a four-game sweep. The *Star Ledger*'s Rich Chere picked the Rangers in six.

Those who anticipated a Ranger blowout in Game One at Madison Square Garden were sadly mistaken. Despite a two-goal New York advantage, the Devils counterattacked in the third period on a Zdeno Ciger 35-footer that reduced the margin to one. From that point to the end, New Jersey did everything but knot the score. In the end, it was still 2-1, but the Rangers knew then and there that they were in for a series. "I'll guarantee they're far from down and discouraged," opined Rangers goalie John Vanbiesbrouck — and he was right on target.

On the New Jersey side, among the more heartening aspects of the loss was Terreri's nimble goaltending. "Chris was great," added Vanbiesbrouck. "He made about five terrific saves early in the game and that enabled his guys to get going."

The Fight At The End Of The Tunnel resumed at the Garden on April 21. Any thoughts the Rangers harbored about a sweep were dramatically put to rest in a collison of forces that would set the tone for the remainder of the competition. Although

Claude Lemieux rose to the occasion all year, then shut down Messier in the playoffs.

Vanbiesbrouck took a 9-0-1 record into the game, the Devils showed him no respect.

Overcoming an early 1-0 Rangers lead, the Devils were never headed after rookie Kevin Todd tied the count. With the score deadlocked at 2-2 in the middle frame, Claude Lemieux and Laurie Boschman scored 56 seconds apart, catapulting New Jersey to an emphatic 7-3 triumph. Significantly, Guerin gave the Devils a three-goal cushion 32 seconds into the third period. It was his first NHL goal.

More than anything, it was Lemieux's two-way game that sparked the win. Claude effectively manacled Messier and scored a pair while he was at it. "Claude played great," said Scott Stevens. "He did a terrific job taking players off and looked exactly like he did when Montreal won the Stanley Cup."

To which Lemieux replied, "It takes four games to win. We played pretty good in the first game, better in the second and we'll have to keep playing better. In this series playing against Messier's line is a big challenge for our line. If we do a good job it inspires the whole team."

For sure, the Devils were an inspired team when they returned home for Game Three. The *New York Times'* Alex Yannis echoed the sentiments of more than 19,000 witnesses when he asserted, "The Devils have converted themselves into a relentlessly fearless and unified team. They played like a team possessed, hitting everything that moved and stood up for each other as if they were family."

Hobbled with a knee injury that would disturb him throughout the series, Richer nevertheless freed himself enough to beat Mike Richter between the pads with a wrist shot at 8:50 of the first period. Mark Messier briefly tied the score at one before Scott Stevens followed with a deflection of a Peter Stastny shot to give the Devils a 2-1 margin.

The backbreaker was provided by Devils left wing Claude Vilgrain. The Haitian-born forward, who had come into his own as a regular in 1991-92, drilled an unscreened, seemingly-handleable shot from along the right boards early in the second period. "I lost sight of it," admitted Richter. "You can't let that happen in a playoff game." But it had happened and it was sufficient for the Devils who preserved the 3-1 lead. New Jersey now led the series two games to one.

If Slava Fetisov had played a better game in the NHL, few could remember when. He disposed of Ranger after Ranger at the blueline. The 34-year-old dished out a number of heavy-but-clean bodychecks and bodyblocked four shots. "These are special games because we are playing the Rangers," a smiling Fetisov explained in the dressing room. "I play physical because that is the way we must play to beat the Rangers."

Vilgrain: "It was inspirational for us the way he played."

As for the Rangers, they knew exactly what had to be done. "We've got to win one game in New Jersey," said coach Roger Neilson. "We played as well as we can play."

"The next game is a must game for us," added Brian Leetch.

And so it was. A Devils win would give them a stranglehold three-games-to-one series lead in The Lincoln Tunnel Tangle.

Game Four drew the usual 19,040 who witnessed a pulsating 0-0 tie through two periods of excrutiatingly tight play. In so many cases such as this, the first goal is much like a sudden-death score, and for a time it appeared as if the Devils would produce just such a red light. "We had more chances in this game than in any previous game," said Stevens.

Number One on the Hockey Bromide List proclaims that it is "a game of mistakes."

Thus, it was a communications breakdown that led to the Devils' desmise. Just past the four minute mark in the third period, New Jersey mounted an attack that was blunted by New York. The Stastny line, which was tiring and needed a respite, still had control of the puck in the Rangers' zone. Peter cradled the rubber on his stick and elected to retain control rather than leave it for the foe. He headed back toward neutral ice when he spotted Fetisov on the right side near the New Jersey blueline.

Stastny dispatched the puck to Fetisov, who was backpedalling at the time. Ordinarily it would have been a successful time-killer, enabling a line change to take place, but this time there was a flaw; the pass lacked zip and never reached its destination. Messier, who was in full flight, intercepted the pass and rapidly sent the rubber cross-ice to Jan Erixon alone in the slot. Erixon found an opening between Terreri's pads at 4:14 of the third. The goal was all the Rangers needed. Try as they might, the Devils could not beat Mike Richter on this night. New York scored two more times and tied the series at two on the strength of the 3-0 margin.

"We had lots of chances," Lemieux concluded, "but Richter stood on his head. If we play the same way I'm sure we'll get a few by him."

The scene shifted to Madison Square Garden for Game Five, which turned out to be the most curious of the opening round and, in the end, betrayed the Devils' need for injured Craig Billington. For starters, the Rangers leaped into a 5-0 lead, sending Terreri to the showers. McVie inserted inexperienced Brodeur into the breach, and relentlessly the Devils worked their way back in the game. One-two-three-four — New Jersey had pushed to within a goal of tying the count and came within a whisker of making it 5-5. Unfortunately, 19-year-old

Brodeur was victimized thereafter. "I should have had the last two (seventh and eighth) by Adam Graves," Brodeur admitted.

Perhaps, but there was no retrieving them. The final score was 8-5 for New York and three-two in games. No question, the loss pained the Devils, but their stirring comeback from the 0-5 deficit fueled hope. "I think we showed them something," said Driver.

The words were translated into actions when the teams took the ice for Game Six — potentially the finale — at the Meadowlands. As expected, the Rangers came on strong, hoping to deliver the coup de grace. Their attacks were repulsed, and then Peter Stastny, who remarkably recovered from a late-season virus, put the Devils ahead, 1-0, on a spectacular breakaway. In time his line would account for four goals and two assists.

A power play goal by Tony Amonte gave the Devils pause, and then they took another blow when Tie Domi beat Terreri at 4:09 of the second period. Instead of gloom enveloping the New Jersey bench, a spirit of combativeness gripped McVie's skaters, and within five minutes they had tied the count. Valeri Zelepukin, the gifted Russian who was a catalyst earlier in the season, returned to form and catapulted Claude Lemieux into the clear with a perfect pass. Claude made good on his breakway at 8:49.

The game proceeded in uncertain see-saw fashion with the lead changing hands as Kevin Todd put New Jersey ahead at 11:10 on a galvanic slapshot. A constant threat to the Jerseyites was the vaunted Rangers power play. It struck forcefully at 15:03 when Brian Leetch cruised deep in the Devils' zone to beat Terreri.

This could have been a deflating moment, but the Devils simply would not be denied on this night. In the next sequence of offensive action, Lemieux once again set the Blueshirts back on their heels. He moved the puck into the Ranger zone, drawing Messier and Leetch to him before releasing his shot. Richter, who was well out of his goal, made the save but Zdeno Ciger grabbed the rebound and sent it into the twine. The time was 15:43.

Jersey rooters wondered whether their club could hang on to the lead. Terreri, wonderful in goal, clearly was hurting but continued to play gallantly as did his defense. Late in the second period the Rangers fired volley after volley at Terreri, but he held fast although at the buzzer he had difficulty moving.

The indomitable goalie would not allow another score the rest of the night. Meanwhile, his teammates relentlessly chipped away at the Rangers' defense and finally obtained the breathing room they sought when Lemieux seized a Messier giveaway and passed out to Stastny, who buried the rubber to make it 5-3.

That was it. The Devils had done what virtually nobody in the media thought possible; they had extended the Rangers to a seventh and final game while winning the hearts of Metropolitan Area hockey fans with heroes galore. Stastny was plus-seven and collected his 100th career playoff point; Lemieux thoroughly outplayed Messier, whose line was minus-eight, and Terreri pushed his endurance to the very limit.

What was an otherwise glorious evening for the Byrne troops was marred at game's end while New Jersey players gathered around winning goalie Chris Terreri. Instead of returning to their dressing room, Rangers brawlers Tie Domi and Joe Kocur approached Laurie Boschman and sucker-punched him. With that, a brawl erupted. When the dust had cleared, it was apparent that the New Jersey-New York rivalry had reached white-heat intensity. "The teams

do not like each other," said Rangers defenseman James Patrick in what must have been the understatement of the series.

So, it was back to Manhattan for Game Seven amid a truly delightful media circus. Columnists such as Mike Lupica, Dave Anderson and Joe Gergen turned away from baseball and focused on the Devils-Rangers series. "You heard it everywhere," wrote Anderson in *The New York Times,* "aren't the playoffs terrific? Will the Devils eliminate the Rangers?"

To do so they would have to win the war of attrition; and in that area they were slipping fast. From goal to the front line, aces were wounded. Spectacular though he was in Game Six, Terreri emerged with a still ailing back. Richer, whose cannon was badly needed on the attack, skated with extreme difficulty because of a gimpy knee. But nothing was more disturbing than the news that Slava Fetisov, who had become a defense force in the series, was hors de combat. A leg injury suffered in the sixth match made it impossible for him to skate. Slava was scratched from the lineup.

"They expected us to be done after the fifth game," said captain Driver, "Nobody figured us to go this far."

If the showdown game was a roulette wheel and the Devils' spin wound up with the worst possible drop of the ball, that would pretty much sum up the luck of the final test. "It seemed," said McVie, "that whatever could go wrong went wrong."

Actually, Game Seven had three parts. In Part One the Devils skated head to head with New York and, at times, had the advantage although the Rangers grabbed a 1-0 lead. Defenseman Tommy Albelin tied the score with a long shot at 3:58 of the first period, and the teams remained tied for more than five minutes of terribly exciting back-and-fourth play.

Then, it happened. While pinning the

Rangers in their defensive zone, Boschman made the mistake of taking a blatant holding penalty at 9:12. Under the circumstances, it was an unnecessary hold and it would cost the Devils dearly. With Boschman in the box, Mike Gartner put the Rangers ahead 2-1. This was followed by yet another New York power play goal at 12:33. At the end of one period it was 3-1 for the Rangers.

"We were matching them hit for hit," said Kevin Todd, "but we just ran out of shots."

Before the Devils could stop the bleeding, it was 6-1 for the Rangers by the 14-minute point of the middle period. Still, the Devils refused to quit. Bill Guerin beat Vanbiesbrouck at 18:49. Lemieux reduced the margin to 6-3 at 7:55 of the third, and then another daredevil rally appeared in the works when Pat Conacher notched a short-hander at 10:10. But at 13:01 New Jersey was nailed for having too many men on the ice.

That did it. The Rangers responded with a power play goal to make it 7-4 and then added an empty-netter. The 1991-92 season offically ended for New Jersey when the buzzer sounded. The 8-4 defeat was difficult to swallow but did not leave the Devils demoralized. "There is no need for the Devils to hang their heads in shame," noted Hugh Delano of *The Post*. "They gave it their best shot. They forced the Rangers, the team with the best record in the NHL, to play seven hard-fought games before winning.

Unhappy with the final results, Lou Lamoriello nevertheless stuck a note of optimism. "We're headed in the right direction," said the club's leader.

Though the season had ended for the Devils, when the Penguins repeated as Stanley Cup champions it served notice that the Patrick Division would remain the premier unit in the league. It was imperative that the Devils keep pace. With that in mind, significant off-season moves would be made.

19

THE BROOKS EXPERIMENT 1992-93

It was a wrenching decision but it was one that Lou Lamoriello believed had to be made; and he delivered the change. Anticipating a more technologically-oriented NHL and one that would place more emphasis on European-style weave-skating, the Devils' leader removed Tom McVie from coaching duties and replaced him with 1980 American Olympic Gold Medal leader Herb Brooks.

"This coaching change should not be construed as an indictment of the job Tom McVie did for us," said Lamoriello. "He served the Devils' organization well for a long period of time, but at present, with the type of talent our team possesses, we find that Herb Brooks is the man best suited to take our team to the top. Tommy did a good job for us last season. It is our belief, however, that at this point in time the Devils have an opportunity to become one of the NHL's premier teams, and that this move is necessary to help us accomplish our goals.

Brooks was enthusiastically greeted by both players and the media at training camp in September 1993. BROOKS STILL RADICAL AFTER ALL THESE YEARS headlined the Star-Ledger in an effusive commentary on the coach's endless quest for innovation.

How radical was Herb?

"I never even burned my draft card," kidded Herb after putting his skaters through the pre-season paces.

Under the Brooks' baton, the Devils emerged as a solid, competitive club in a Patrick Division that was sizzling with parity. Meanwhile, Lamoriello sought a deal that would give his outfit an edge and concluded that it had to be at center.

After three months of discussions with an assortment of general managers, Lamoriello filled a center ice gap by dealing Zdeno Ciger and Kevin Todd to the Edmonton Oilers for Bernie Nicholls.

The mid-January 1993 trade made a lot of sense. Neither the youthful Todd nor Czech-born Ciger had played up to their early notices. They were used sparingly and became eminently expendable. In Nicholls,

Bernie Nicholls was a welcomed addition to the Devils' lineup in January, 1993.

the Devils were fortified with an accomplished pivot who was equally adept at scoring and playmaking.

"Bernie gives us a dimension we did not have," the president asserted, "a dimension that makes us a better team, and he is a proven scorer."

Certainly, the media response was warm. Writing in The Record, John Dellapina cited nine (as in Nicholls' number) different ways Bernie would benefit the home club. The New York Post's Hugh Delano enthused, "Lamoriello's 24th trade since he took over as Devils' g.m. in 1987 could be his best."

Every piece had appeared to have fallen into place. Goaltending and defense were solid and now, with Nicholls diversifying the attack, New Jersey ranked among the NHL's best-balanced squads.

It was late January and no news was more distressing to the club as a whole— and Bernie Nicholls in particular—than word from Long Beach, California that Jake Nicholls was hospitalized with spinal meningitis.

The infant son of Heather and Bernie Nicholls had been born November 25, 1992 with Downs Syndrome and now the two-month old was in critical condition. Nicholls flew to his son's bedside in a Long Beach hospital.

"Obviously, the baby is his first priority," said Brooks. "It's a hard one, but I feel Bernie will be okay. He knows the frailty of life. I have an awful lot of admiration for people who go through trying times."

As Jake Nicholls would battle to stay alive, Bernie would criss-cross the country whenever possible to be with his son. His distraction from the hockey scene was perfectly natural and completely understood by fans and teammates alike.

As expected, Pittsburgh ran away with the Patrick Division crown while Washington edged the Islanders out of the runner-up spot. The Devils pulled up the playoff rear as the four Patrick Division Playoff teams prepared for the quest for the Stanley Cup.

It meant that New Jersey would open

against Pittsburgh and, as The Record's Terry Egan opined, "Looking forward to playing the Penguins is like looking forward to paying taxes."

The opening round premiered in Pittsburgh on April 18, 1992 and Penguins' power prevailed. The score was 6-3 for Pittsburgh in a game where Brooks' stick-handlers simply could not put a blanket over the home team's guns. A day's rest provided no respite. In Game Two, Lemieux & Co. scored seven unanswered goals to nothing for the visitors.

Game Three was anything but a rout — Pittsburgh prevailed, 4-3 — and there was much to commend on the home side; except for the decision. Down by three games, the Devils had their pride on the line.

If there was redemption, it came on Sunday afternoon, April 25, 1993. Stephane Richer beat goalie Tom Barrasso on a power play goal early in the first period and Tommy Albelin added another power play red light late in the second. When Claude Lemieux made it 3-0 — yet another power play job — the roaring Byrne Arena crowd knew this game was in the bag. And it was, to the tune of 4-1 Devils.

Despite the one-game-to-three deficit, the Devils camp began bubbling with optimism as the scene shifted back to Pittsburgh for Game Five. Suddenly, Lemieux was stoppable and Barrasso was beatable. "Hey, another win and we go back home again," was the prevailing theme in the Devils' dressing room.

New Jersey's shooters carried that theme right on to The Civic Center ice. Despite a 2-0 Pittsburgh lead in the first period Brooks gleefully watched as his men tallied three unanswered goals to close the middle frame with a 3-2 lead.

For more than five minutes into period three, the Devils kept the lid on Pittsburgh's generator and had the situation well in hand until Penguins' rookie Martin Straka assaulted New Jersey's net.

"Straka stepped on my stick," moaned Terreri, "and fell down. There shouldn't have been a penalty."

But there was. Referee Don Koharski — he of Donut infamy — whistled Scott Stevens off for two minutes, setting the Penguins' power play in motion.

Although John Dellapina, now writing for The Daily News, termed the call "a phantom hook," Koharski was not about to alter his decision and the New Jersey penalty-killers took the ice.

For 90 seconds, they kept the marauders at bay but Ron Francis corralled the rubber at the right circle and delivered a slap shot that eyed its way through Terreri's pads to tie the count.

"It was a terrible call," said Stevens. "It changed the outcome of the game and gave them momentum. They can fine me or do whatever they want because it was just a terrible call. I still don't know what he saw out there."

Stevens was right on all counts. The tide had turned and within minutes Jeff Daniels thrust Pittsburgh into the lead, grabbing the rebound of a Dave Tippett shot out of the air, dropping it to his feet whereupon he beat Terreri to the glove side.

Try as they might, the Devils were unable to close the deficit and, with Terreri removed for a sixth attacker, Pittsburgh closed the series when Daniels scored into the open net at 18:59.

Clearly, the wheels in the high command were turning. Neither the owner nor the general manager were satisfied with the results and changes certainly would be made.

But where?

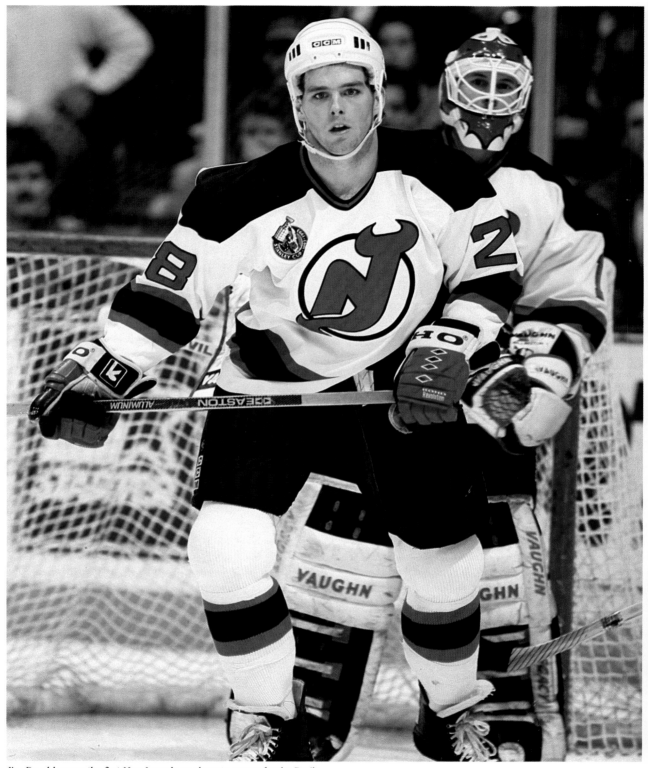

Jim Dowd became the first New Jersey-born player to appear for the Devils.

20

ENTER
JACQUES LEMAIRE
1993-94

In the wake of the Devils playoff defeat it was inevitable that the media post mortems would focus on two pivotal issues; was the team capable of an even better performance? And, if so, would it perform in a more superior manner under another coach?

But who would be an adequate replacement; the man who could lift the Devils to the next level?

Lamoriello knew who he wanted but wasn't certain whether he was obtainable. Jacques Lemaire had an outstanding record behind the bench on the university level as well as in Junior hockey and the NHL, with the Montreal Canadiens. Now a member of the Habs' high command, Lemaire was a valued and treasured associate of Montreal's general manager Serge Savard.

When Lemaire unequivocally assured Lamoriello that he wanted to coach again, Lou approached Savard and persuaded his colleague to release Jacques.

During the half-hour before the news meeting had begun nobody had a clue who would accompany Lamoriello to the podium. As the journalists focused on the head table, the president emerged from the hallway and strutted to the forefront with a smiling, effevescent man at his side. To everyone's astonishment, Jacques Lemaire was named head coach.

"He brings impeccable credentials to the Devils which are recognized throughout the entire NHL," Lamoriello told the packed crowd. "His reputation and knowledge have earned him a high level of respect from everyone he comes in contact with, including management personnel, members of the media, and most importantly from NHL players.

"When combined with an unmistakable confidence, and his clear-cut expertise and poise, the assets he possesses will leave no doubt as to his level of authority in our dressing room."

Lemaire wasted no time building his staff. He imported Hall of Fame defenseman Larry Robinson as his assistant coach and persuaded the erudite former NHL goaltender Jacques Caron to come aboard as the club's new goaltending professor.

Unquestionably, the focus was on Lemaire and the immediate reaction was emphatically positive. With eight Stanley Cup rings not to mention Hall of Fame credentials, Jacques was unlike any benchmaster the Devils ever boasted.

"He will command instant respect the moment he walks into the lockerroom," Lamoriello promised.

When training camp opened early in September 1993, Lemaire immediately put a system into place and would religiously retain it throughout the campaign. "I believe that to win, you've got to play pretty good defensively," Jacques asserted. "One of my first steps will be to show how to play in our zone and the neutral zone. We have a good mixture of veterans and young defensemen."

Finding the proper combinations required constant adding of ingredients, blending, examination and, often, more stirring after that. Lemaire was certain of one aspect; as much as possible he sought roster stability and established lines.

"I believe that when three guys know each other well and know what they'll do and where they'll go, they will play better than if you're switching all the time," Lemaire explained.

Peter Sidorkiewicz, who Lamoriello obtained from Ottawa along with forward Mike Peluso, had suffered a shoulder injury in the final game of the 1992-93 season. The Devils had been misinformed (for which the NHL later would award compensation) by the Senators' management about the goaltender's condition and when it was revealed that a long recuperation was required, Lemaire had to find a replacement. His choice—a fortunate one, as it would happen—was Martin Brodeur. But, for the moment, Chris Terreri was number one.

The enthusiasm of training camp had immediate carry-over value for the new season. From the top-liners to the borderline skaters, from rookies to career Devils such as defenseman Ken Daneyko, praise for Lemaire was unanimous.

"When he walked in here, Jacques got instant respect," said Daneyko. "You couldn't help but respect him. He comes from a winning organization. He was a winner in Montreal and when he speaks, you know what he's talking about.

The positive talk was converted to positive action. One, two, three, four, five, six, seven straight victories to start the 1993-94 season. Under Lemaire, New Jersey already had set a franchise record to open the campaign. They beat the Florida Panthers, 2-1, on October 24, 1993 to establish the mark but there was more to the game than that.

Bruce Driver, one of the senior Devils and one of the most insightful, credited the successful training camp with putting the club on track. "We had good preparation," said the defenseman. "Jacques and Larry came in and told us how they wanted us to play."

Game Eight was not against just any other team; the opponents would be the Stanley Cup champion Montreal Canadiens, the alma mater of Lemaire and Robinson.

As early season games go, it was a gem and for the home club, a good litmus test. Montreal won 2-0 but the Devils completely outplayed the visitors, losing only because of a world-class effort by Canadiens' goaltender Patrick Roy.

The bottom line was that the Devils were at the top. They had moved to the next level that Lamoriello had sought when he hired Lemaire.

There were many reasons, the team orientation being among them. New Jersey was less a club of individual stars and glitzy braggadocio and more a unit that became the quintessential example of togetherness.

Although New Jersey boasted one of the best defensive records in the NHL, the concept of four-line balance — and freshness — had catapulted the Devils to the top rung among scoring teams as well. Somehow, Lemaire had discovered the ideal formula, yet he remained suitably cautious through the final weeks.

Better than any team New Jersey has known. The Devils completed the 84-game schedule with 47 wins, 25 losses and 12 ties for a club record total of 106 points.

Lamoriello's choice of June 28, 1993 had become the genius selection nine months later. "He is the best coach I've ever played for, and it's not even close," said Terreri. "He's so good that sometimes it's scary."

Scott Stevens: "I've never been on a team before where, when the coach is talking, everybody looks at him and listens.

The local media, never known to miss a critical opportunity, lavished praise on Lemaire as it had on no other coach in franchise history.

One issue that consumed Lemaire as he prepared his club for the opening playoff round challenge from Buffalo was which goaltender to start against the Sabres.

Brodeur, the rookie sensation, had a 27-11-8 record with a 2.40 goals against average and .915 save percentage. The veteran Terreri had equally impressive numbers (20-11-4, 2.72, .907) as well as the benefit of vast playoff experience.

Lemaire chose Brodeur but he examined his club beyond the goaltending. These were the playoffs, a new milieu for his skaters and he wondered. "If we lose the first game," he mused, "how are we going to react? Do we have a player who will put

himself on the line by saying something to the others? I honestly don't know because I haven't had them in that situation.

They did lose the opener, 2-0, at the Meadowlands. Dominik Hasek, the NHL's top-ranking goaltender, threw a wall in front of his net and totally frustrated the Devils. Game Two would go a long way toward revealing the strength of New Jersey's fibre.

For Lemaire, the response could not have been more gratifying. His stickhandlers responded nobly with a 2-1 victory and then beat the Sabres by the same score in Buffalo. Game Four went to the home team, 5-3 as the teams returned to East Rutherford with the series knotted at two apiece.

Despite the Devils 5-3 triumph at home — Lemaire's men now had a three-game-to-two lead — the series was far from over.

The night of April 27, 1994 — and early morning of April 28 — will remain etched in NHL annals among the most stirring in league history. For three periods of end-to-end, tough-checking, vintage playoff hockey, New Jersey and Buffalo battled at the ancient Auditorium. Both Brodeur and Hasek were invulnerable and the score registered 0-0 after regulation time had expired.

As the Aud's clock ticked past the Midnight mark, the teams were locked in combat. For a fleeting moment it appeared that Bobby Carpenter might have the winner on his stick; then Stephane Richer, but the Devils were foiled again by Hasek.

And so it was a fourth overtime period. Players from both sides were so exhausted they often appeared to be skating in mud, but on and on they went. At last a break. The Sabres moved the puck into the right corner of Devils' ice. A pass eluded Tommy Albelin stationed in front of Brodeur. The puck skimmed tantalizingly to Dave Hannan as

Brodeur attempted to regain position. Too late. Hannan lifted the rubber over the Devils' goaltender at 65:43 of overtime to give Buffalo a 1-0 victory and a three-three tie in games.

"When it gets tough," said Lemaire, "I want to see who's going to get out and push.

In a sense, it was the entire New Jersey club in Game Seven, Friday, April 29, 1994 at the Meadowlands. Buffalo grabbed the essential 1-0 lead but Bruce Driver and Claude Lemieux put the Devils back in the catbird seat and Brodeur was Mister Goalie from that point on. The Byrne scoreboard registered 2-1 for the home team as the final buzzer sounded. Lemaire & Co. had surmounted their first hurdle.

The Devils' dressing room oozed with a quiet confidence as players discussed the immediate past and the impending future series which would open in only two days at home against Boston's always-dangerous Bruins.

To a man the Jerseyites expected to beat the Beantowners but nobody expected it to be easy. Then again, nobody expected to be down two games after the opening couple—Sunday, May 1 and Tuesday, May 3—at home. After Don Sweeney beat Brodeur at 9:08 of overtime in Game Two, the Devils embarked for Boston so far behind the eight-ball, there were those who feared they might be swept in four.

They had the will. They edged Boston, 4-2, to creep within one and then played another classic. On Saturday night, May 7, 1994 they went into overtime again.

The difference in this contest, as it was in the third, could be found in New Jersey's goal. Gambling as he never had all season, Lemaire had inserted New England-born Terreri between the pipes. It was a pressure situation the likes of which no New Jersey goalie ever had faced; and smiling Chris responded with a confidence and crispness

that never will be forgotten.

For most of the first overtime, he was a Horatio at the Bridge, thwarting the Bruins while his mates gasped for second wind. Just past the 24-minute mark, a face-off was held near center ice. Bobby Holik would take the draw against Adam Oates but before doing so, the Devil peered over to the bench. "I got a signal from Larry Robinson to move the puck forward," Holik recalled.

And so he did. The rubber ricochetted past the stunned Bruins while Richer, who also got the signal from Robinson, outflanked the Boston defenders and cruised in alone on Bruins' goalie Jon Casey. "It's the kind of clutch situation I love," Richer later admitted.

Stephane feinted, enticing Casey to lunge for the rubber, then pulled it out of the sprawling goaltender's sphere of grasp and into the yawning net. The goal, scored at 14:19 of overtime, tied the series at two apiece and sent it back to New Jersey where Lemaire had yet another agonizing goaltending decision to make; should he accept the orthodox view and go with the hot hand, Terreri, or counter with Brodeur?

Lemaire chose Brodeur because he was rested and added that Terreri would be in goal for Game Six at Boston, no matter what happened in Jersey. The result: Brodeur pitched a 2-0 shutout.

One win away from a stunning comeback, the Devils returned to Boston and, true to his blueprint, Lemaire replaced Brodeur despite Martin's last shutout. The move drew an intense amount of scrutiny from the press legions which were growing by the game. Jacques' audacity in daring to remove his winning netminder was challenged by traditionalists who argued that it's heresy to break up a successful combination.

There were many heroes in the finale but none more than John MacLean who, in a

John McLean parked in front of the Bruins defense during playoffs.

sense, staked his scoring reputation on the 1993-94 season. Nobody could attest to Johnny Mac's clutch-ability more than Bruins' goalie Jon Casey who was beaten twice by the doughty right wing. "It was like old times," said MacLean, and every Devils fan knew what he meant, Final score: New Jersey, 5 Boston, 3.

"I'm very proud of them," said Lamoriello in the packed and jubilant lockerroom after the game.

And well he should have been, especially for the choice of Lemaire who was toasted throughout the Bruins' dressing room as well as his own. "Jacques pushed all the right buttons," said Boston defenseman Gordie Roberts. "He puts Ben Hankinson in Game Four and he scores a goal. He puts Corey Millen in Game Five and he gets a

goal. He goes back to Terreri in Game Six and he wins it for them. That's quite a parlay."

Asked about his decision-making, Lemaire merely smiled modestly and quipped, "None of the moves are good if we lose. But all the moves, to me, made sense. That's why I did it."

What he did was catapult his club into the Conference finals against the New York Rangers.

Here was a match made in promotional heaven. New York had won The Presidents' Trophy and had been made the favorite to win The Stanley Cup. What's more, the Broadway Blueshirts had won all six of the games played with the Devils during the regular campaign.

"But," noted captain Scott Stevens,

"that was one season and this is a new one."

"We have a great deal of respect for the New Jersey Devils," said Rangers coach Mike Keenan when a reporter suggested that his club might continue its mastery and sweep the series in four.

The respect was well-founded. Down a goal to New York in the opener and seemingly out, the Lemaireites refused to wilt. With Martin Brodeur replaced by a sixth skater, the Devils stormed the Rangers zone in the final minute and tied the score when Claude Lemieux knocked the puck past Mike Richter from a scramble in front.

Once again, the stage was set for Stephane Richer's magic stick and it delivered. Having soiled a Brian Leetch assault after 35:18 of sudden death, Bobby Carpenter flipped a delicate pass to Richer along the left boards. With only Adam Graves between him and Richter, Richer went into overdrive, outflanked Graves and flipped the rubber over Richter just as the goalie attempted his pokecheck. The red light flashed at 35:23 of overtime.

There were many ramifications of the 4-3 New Jersey triumph but, most of all, it served notice to one and all that the Devils were prepared to give their rivals from Manhattan an intense run for their money.

Not that the Rangers didn't expect it. They sprinted from the gate in the opening minutes for Game Two at the Garden, scored an early goal and then repeatedly repulsed the onrushing Devils. The score remained 1-0 into the third period but Lemaire's shooters couldn't find the opening and eventually New York pulled ahead to win 4-0.

One thing was certain, an immensely entertaining and pulsating series was now well underway even outdoing its early promise. Game Three fulfilled the script with yet another Devils comeback and more

overtime. But this time the other team won. Stephane Matteau swatted a loose puck which found its way through the labyrinth of legs and behind Brodeur at 26:13 of overtime.

Everyone agreed that Game Four would set the tone for the rest of the series. A Rangers win would put the Devils in a precarious position whereas if the home club could tie the count, hey, anything could happen.

It was a vintage win for the Devs. Brodeur was immense; the defense had a Gibralter-like quality and the forwards, when not tending to their checking, sallied forth and produced three goals to only one for the visitors.

Devils' optimism was on the rise. They returned to Manhattan and spanked the Rangers, 4-1, in a game which they led, 4-0, until late in the third period.

One game away from the Stanley Cup finals, the Devils nevertheless were not getting the media space that one would have expected under the circumstances. Much attention was given the Rangers' front office turmoil instead and, in a rare display of displeasure, Lemaire took the press to task.

"I want my players to get the recognition they deserve," he said. "They never get the credit (from the media) when they win. Our guys deserve more when you consider what they achieved."

Having said that, he turned his attention to Game Six, Wednesday, May 25, 1994 at Bynre Arena. It was a contest filled with amazing twists and turns but one with a single constant; excitement throughout.

The capacity crowd of 19,040 was treated to a first period which was dominated by the home club. New Jersey exited with a 2-0 lead on goals by Niedermayer and Lemieux. Every aspect of Lemaire's game plan was working, a fact not overlooked by the New

Yorkers. They were a dispirited lot heading to their dressing room and it was reflected in the first half of the second period. Wave after wave of Devils poured through the Rangers defensive lines hurling innumerable volleys at Richter. The third — and very likely series-crushing — goal appeared imminent. But, alas, it never came.

Still, if New Jersey could carry a two-goal lead to the dressing room with 20 minutes remaining, it was a desirable scenario. However, one mix-up allowed Alexei Kovalev a bit of skating room and the sharpshooting Ranger rifled a shot past Brodeur. Instead of a three-goal cushion, the Devils had to contend with a fragile one-goal lead going into the third period.

Sure enough, the Rangers broke loose for three unanswered third period goals to annex the game, 4-2. For the Devils it was a devastating loss, but would it be so severe as to ruin them for Game Seven at the Garden. That was the primary question and, once again, Devils' fortitude would come to the forefront.

Like Game Six, Game Seven is now regarded as one of the finest playoff games in the NHL's long history. The Rangers took an early lead and carefully defended Richter's one-goal margin through the first, second and most of the third periods. Still, Devils fought back and finally removed Brodeur for a last desperate effort.

The final thrust began with Nicholls winning a face-off in the New York end. Suddenly, a play was in motion that culminated with Valeri Zelepukin camping in front of the net in position to deposit the puck behind Richter with only seven seconds remaining on the clock! It was an overtime get again.

"I told my players to be patient," said Lemaire, "and not make any mistakes that would give the Rangers a scoring opportunity."

At one point, the Devils appeared to have the winner. Richter skated to his right boards to field a loose puck but, somehow, Billy Guerin lost sight of the biscuit. By the time he got possession, the Rangers net was covered and the threat nullified, enabling the game to grind into a second overtime.

An attempted Devils clearing pass was retrieved by Matteau who moved down the left side and then swerved behind the net. Being checked by Scott Niedermayer, the Ranger attempted a desperation centering pass yet, somehow, the winning goal, thus concluding the Devils' dramatic run for The Cup.

Few teams which came up on the short end of a playoff ever received more across-the-board acclaim than New Jersey did in the aftermath of this remarkable series. Devils' courage, craftmanship, and class were cited among the club's many assets.

Among the proudest in the visitors' dressing room was the club's architect and leader, Lou Lamoriello, who was to be voted general manager of the year by no less a respectful group than his NHL peers. Pumping his players' hands was Dr. John McMullen, the man who personally delivered the franchise to New Jersey.

"I know I'm never going to die of a broken heart or a bad stomach," chuckled Dr. McMullen, "because, if that were the case, it would have happened already."

"Jacques and Larry have inspired the guys. It's a team with a minimum amount of ego and that's all to the credit of the coaches."

The thrilling playoff efforts against Buffalo, Boston and New York have given the Devils a 14-carat stamp of respectability and provided fans with the confidence that a Stanley Cup is within their grasp.

As Lamoriello cogently concluded, "The best is yet to come."

EPILOGUE
THE FUTURE IS BRIGHT

Pain and progress are inseparable.

Sweet are the uses of adversity.

You can take the best of the bromides and find that they are applicable to New Jersey's hockey club.

It is a franchise which has endured considerable hardship, from the Wayne Gretzky taunts to the agony of playoff defeat.

But it also is a very special franchise. It is not a face-less corporate entity, nor one whose leaders closet themselves out of public view.

In many ways the Devils are the most "family" franchise in the 26-team NHL. The McMullens, John and Peter, are hands-on owners while Lou Lamoriello is a president and general manager as dedicated and hard-working as any who ever graced the league, dating back to the immortal Conn Smythe.

The combined effort resulted in a 1993-94 campaign that was sprinkled with new team records, the Devils' highest standing ever as well as the honor of individual awards.

Jacques Lemaire was voted coach-of-the-year; Scott Stevens was named to The First All-Star Team and came within a hair of being picked for the Norris Trophy. He also topped the entire league in plus-minus; and Martin Brodeur was acclaimed Calder Trophy-winner in a breeze.

Thus, the bottom line is rather obvious. The Devils approach the second half of the decade with more enthusiasm and optimism than ever with a Stanley Cup very much on their minds and within their grasp.

Devils All-Time Leader Board
DEVILS (1982-94)

GAMES PLAYED
1. John MacLean* 706
2. Ken Daneyko* 691
3. Bruce Driver* 661
4. Aaron Broten 581
5. Kirk Muller 556
6. Pat Verbeek 463
7. Joe Cirella 438
8. Doug Brown 350
9. Viacheslav Fetisov 337
10. Claude Lemieux* 308

GOALS
1. John MacLean* 278
2. Kirk Muller 185
3. Pat Verbeek 170
4. Aaron Broten 147
5. Claude Lemieux* 119
6. Stephane Richer* 103
7. Brendan Shanahan 96
8. Mark Johnson 89
9. Doug Sulliman 86
   Patrik Sundstrom 86

ASSISTS
1. Kirk Muller 335
2. Bruce Driver* 304
3. Aaron Broten 283
4. John MacLean* 281
5. Patrik Sundstrom 160

6. Pat Verbeek 151
7. Mel Bridgman 148
8. Joe Cirella 147
   Scott Stevens* 147
10. Mark Johnson 140

POINTS
1. John MacLean* 559
2. Kirk Muller 520
3. Aaron Broten 430
4. Bruce Driver* 383
5. Pat Verbeek 321
6. Patrik Sundstrom 246
7. Claude Lemieux* 240
8. Mark Johnson 229
9. Mel Bridgman 224
10. Brendan Shanahan 214

PENALTY MINUTES
1. Ken Daneyko* 1882
2. John MacLean* 982
3. Pat Verbeek 943
4. Joe Cirella 886
5. Randy McKay* 696
6. David Maley 683
7. Kirk Muller 572
8. Perry Anderson 553
9. Brendan Shanahan 524
10. Bruce Driver 516

GOALTENDING

GAMES PLAYED
1. Chris Terreri* 249
2. Glenn Resch 198
3. Sean Burke 162

MINUTES
1. Chris Terreri* 13789
2. Glenn Resch 10953
3. Sean Burke 9061

SHUTOUTS
1. Chris Terreri* 6
2. Craig Billington 4
   Sean Burke 4

GAA (2 Seasons)
1. Chris Terreri* 3.13
2. Sean Burke 3.66
3. Bob Sauve 3.87

WINS
1. Chris Terreri* 100
2. Sean Burke 62
2. Alain Chevrier 53

TIES
1. Chris Terreri* 34
2. Sean Burke 23
3. Glenn Resch 20

*Current Devils

FRANCHISE (1974-93)

GAMES PLAYED
1. John MacLean* 706
2. Ken Daneyko* 691
3. Bruce Driver* 661
4. Aaron Broten 641
5. Kirk Muller 556
6. Joe Cirella 503
7. Mike Kitchen 474
8. Pat Verbeek 463
9. Wilf Paiement 392
10. Gary Croteau 390

GOALS
1. John MacLean* 278
2. Kirk Muller 185
3. Pat Verbeek 170
4. Aaron Broten 162
5. Wilf Paiement 153
6. Claude Lemieux* 119
7. Paul Gagne 106
8. Stephane Richer* 103
9. Brendan Shanahan 96
10. Gary Croteau 92

ASSISTS
1. Kirk Muller 335
2. Aaron Broten 307
3. Bruce Driver* 304
4. John MacLean* 281
5. Wilf Paiement 183

6. Patrik Sundstrom 160
7. Joe Cirella 159
8. Pat Verbeek 151
9. Mel Bridgman 148
10. Scott Stevens* 147

POINTS
1. John MacLean* 559
2. Kirk Muller 520
3. Aaron Broten 469
4. Bruce Driver* 383
5. Wilf Paiement 336
6. Pat Verbeek 321
7. Patrik Sundstrom 246
8. Claude Lemieux* 240
9. Mark Johnson 229
10. Mel Bridgman 224

PENALTY MINUTES
1. Ken Daneyko* 1882
2. John MacLean* 982
3. Pat Verbeek 943
4. Joe Cirella 938
5. Randy McKay* 969
6. David Maley 683
7. Kirk Muller 572
8. Wilf Paiement 558
9. Perry Anderson 553
10. Rob Ramage 529

GOALTENDING

GAMES PLAYED
1. Glenn Resch 267
2. Chris Terreri* 249
3. Sean Burke 162

MINUTES
1. Glenn Resch 14826
2. Chris Terreri* 13789
3. Sean Burke 9061

SHUTOUTS
1. Chris Terreri* 6
2. Craig Billington 4
   Sean Burke 4

GAA (2 Seasons)
1. Chris Terreri* 3.13
2. Sean Burke 3.66
3. Bob Sauve 3.87

WINS
1. Chris Terreri* 100
2. Glenn Resch 67
3. Sean Burke 62

TIES
1. Chris Terreri* 34
2. Glenn Resch 33
3. Michel Plasse 25

*Current Devils

196

DEVILS-SINGLE SEASON

GAMES PLAYED

1. Ken Daneyko* (1992-93) 84
2. Scott Stevens* (1993-94 83
   Bruce Driver* (1992-93) 83
4. Valeri Zelepukin* (1993-94) 82
   Alexander Semak* (1992-93) 82
6. Bill Guerin* (1993-94) 81
   Scott Niedermayer* (1993-94) 81
   Scott Stevens* (1992-93) 81
9. 27 tied with 80

GOALS

1. Pat Verbeek (1987-88) 46
2. John MacLean* (1990-91) 45
3. John MacLean* (1988-89) 42
4. Claude Lemieux* (1991-92) 41
   John MacLean* (1989-90) 41
6. Stephane Richer* (1992-93) 38
7. John MacLean* (1993-94) 37
   Alexander Semak* (1992-93) 37
9. Kirk Muller (1987-88) 37
10. Stephane Richer* (1993-94) 36

ASSISTS

1. Scott Stevens* (1993-94) 60
2. Aaron Broten (1987-88) 57
   Kirk Muller (1987-88) 57
4. Kirk Muller (1989-90) 56
5. Aaron Broten (1986-87) 53

6. Claude Lemieux* (1992-93) 51
   Kirk Muller (1990-91) 51
8. Tom Kurvers (1988-89) 50
   Kirk Muller (1986-87) 50
10. Patrik Sundstrom (1989-90) 49

POINTS

1. Kirk Muller (1987-88) 94
2. John MacLean* (1988-89) 87
3. Kirk Muller (1989-90) 86
4. Aaron Broten (1987-88) 83
5. Claude Lemieux* (1992-93) 81
6. John MacLean* (1989-90) 79
   Aaron Broten (1986-87) 79
8. Scott Stevens* (1993-94) 78
   John MacLean* (1990-91) 78
10. Two Tied With 77

PENALTY MINUTES

1. Ken Daneyko* (1988-89) 283
2. Ken Daneyko* (1990-91) 249
   David Maley (1988-89) 249
4. Randy McKay* (1991-92) 246
5. Randy McKay* (1993-94) 244
6. Ken Daneyko* (1987-88) 239
7. Mike Peluso* (1993-94) 238
8. Ken Daneyko* (1992-93) 236
9. Pat Verbeek (1987-88) 227
10. Perry Anderson (1987-88) 222

GOALTENDING

GAMES PLAYED

1. Glenn Resch (1982-83) 65
2. Sean Burke (1988-89) 62
3. Alain Chevrier (1986-87) 58

MINUTES

1. Glenn Resch (1986-87) 3650
2. Sean Burke (1988-89) 3590
3. Chris Terreri* (1991-92) 3185

*Current Devils

SHUTOUTS
1. Martin Brodeur* (1993-94) 3
   Sean Burke (1988-89) 3
3. Four Tied With 2

WINS
1. Martin Brodeur* (1993-94) 27
2. Chris Terreri* (1990-91) 24
   Alain Chevrier (1986-87) 24

GAA (27 GP)
1. Martin Brodeur* (1993-94) 2.40
2. Chris Terreri* (1993-94) 2.72
3. Chris Terreri* (1990-91) 2.91

TIES
1. Glenn Resch (1982-83) 12
2. Chris Terreri* (1991-92) 10
3. Sean Burke (1988-89) 9

*Current Devils

SEASON RECORDS 1982-1994

YEAR BY YEAR

SEASON	GP	W	L	T	PTS	PCT	GF	GA	FINISH
1982-83	80	17	49	14	48	.300	230	338	5
1983-84	80	17	56	7	41	.256	231	350	5
1984-85	80	22	48	10	54	.338	264	346	5
1985-86	80	28	49	3	59	.369	300	374	6
1986-87	80	29	45	6	64	.400	293	368	6
1987-88	80	38	36	6	82	.513	295	296	4
1988-89	80	27	41	12	66	.413	281	325	5
1989-90	80	37	34	9	83	.519	295	288	2
1990-91	80	32	33	15	79	.494	272	264	4
1991-92	80	38	31	11	87	.544	289	259	4
1992-93	84	40	37	7	87	.518	308	299	4
1993-94	84	47	25	12	106	.631	306	220	*2/3
Totals	968	372	484	112	856	.442	3364	3727	—

*Includes Division/Conference Rank.

HOME AND AWAY

	HOME							AWAY						
SEASON	GP	W	L	T	TS	GF	GA	GP	W	L	T	PTS	GF	GA
1982-83	40	11	20	9	31	124	156	40	6	29	5	17	106	182
1983-84	40	10	28	2	22	114	167	40	7	28	5	19	117	183
1984-85	40	13	21	6	32	138	158	40	9	27	4	22	126	188
1985-86	40	17	21	2	36	156	170	40	11	28	1	23	144	204
1986-87	40	20	17	3	43	155	164	40	9	28	3	21	138	204
1987-88	40	23	16	1	47	151	132	40	15	20	5	35	144	164
1988-89	40	17	18	5	39	143	149	40	10	23	7	27	138	176
1989-90	40	22	15	3	47	140	123	40	15	19	6	36	155	165
1990-91	40	23	10	7	53	147	115	40	9	23	8	26	125	149
1991-92	40	24	12	4	52	155	115	40	14	19	7	35	134	144
1992-93	42	24*	14	4	52	165	131	42	16	23*	3	35	143	168
1993-94	42	29*	11	2	60	160	99	42	18	14*	10	46	146	121
Totals	484	233	203	48	514	1748	1679	484	139	281	64	342	1616	2048

*Includes Neutral Site Games.

DIVISIONAL

	OWN DIVISION							OTHER DIVISIONS						
SEASON	GP	W	L	T	PTS	GF	GA	GP	W	L	T	PTS	GF	GA
1982-82	35	8	22	5	21	96	146	45	9	27	9	27	134	192
1983-84	35	4	28	3	11	85	153	45	13	28	4	30	146	197
1984-85	35	14	18	3	31	127	144	45	8	30	7	23	137	202
1985-86	35	10	24	1	21	118	160	45	18	25	2	38	182	214
1986-87	35	13	21	1	27	133	171	45	16	24	5	37	160	197
1987-88	35	19	14	2	40	141	124	45	19	22	4	42	154	172
1988-89	35	12	19	4	28	130	151	45	15	22	8	38	151	174
1989-90	35	18	12	5	41	140	118	45	19	22	4	42	155	170
1990-91	35	13	16	6	32	117	126	45	19	17	9	47	155	138
1991-92	35	14	16	5	33	120	126	45	24	15	6	54	169	133
1992-93	37	18	17	2	38	125	141	47	22	20	5	49	183	158
1993-94	31	17	11	3	37	101	91	53	30	14	9	69	205	129
Totals	418	160	218	40	360	1433	1651	550	212	266	72	496	1931	2076

CLUB LEADERS

SEASON	GOALS		ASSISTS		POINTS		PIM	
1982-83	Tambellini	25	Levo	40	Broten	55	Vautour	136
1983-84	Bridgman	23	Bridgman	38	Bridgman	61	Verbeek	158
1984-85	Gagne	24	Pichette	40	Bridgman	61	Verbeek	162
1985-86	Adams	35	Adams	42	Adams	77	Cirella	147
1986-87	Verbeek	35	Broten	53	Broten	79	Daneyko	183
1987-88	Verbeek	46	Muller	57	Muller	94	Daneyko	239
			Broten	57				
1988-89	MacLean	42	Kurvers	50	MacLean	87	Daneyko	283
1989-90	MacLean	41	Muller	56	Muller	86	Daneyko	219
1990-91	MacLean	45	Muller	51	MacLean	78	Daneyko	249
1991-92	Lemieux	41	Stevens	42	Lemieux	68	McKay	246
			Todd	42				
1992-93	Richer	38	Lemieux	51	Lemieux	81	Daneyko	236
1993-94	MacLean	37	Stevens	60	Stevens	78	McKay	244

SEASON	PPG		SHG		GAA (25 GP)		WINS	
1982-83	Lever	9	Lever	3	Resch	3.98	Resch	15
1983-84	Bridgman	9	McAdam	2	Resch	4.18	Resch	9
1984-85	Broten	10	Bridgman	3	Low	3.84	Resch	15
1985-86	Adams	10	five with	1	Resch	4.27	Chevrier	11
1986-87	Verbeek	17	Brickley	3	Chevrier	4.32	Chevrier	24
1987-88	Muller	17	Brown	4	Sauve	3.56	Chevrier	18
1988-89	MacLean	14	seven with	1	Burke	3.84	Burke	22
1989-90	MacLean	10	MacLean	3	Terreri	3.41	Burke	22
			Brown	3				
1990-91	MacLean	19	three with	2	Terreri	2.91	Terreri	24
1991-92	Lemieux	13	Chorske	3	Billington	3.04	Terreri	22
1992-93	Lemieux	13	Pellerin	2	Terreri	3.39	Billington	21
1993-94	MacLean	8	Richer	3	Brodeur	2.40	Brodeur	27
	Zelepukin	8						

EXECUTIVE PERSONNEL

PRESIDENTS
Bob Butera . . . . April 15, 1983 - April 24, 1987
Lou Lamoriello . . . . April 30, 1987 -

EXECUTIVE VICE PRESIDENT
Max McNab . . . . September 10, 1987 - October 31, 1994

GENERAL MANAGERS
Billy MacMillan . . . . 1982-83 through November 22, 1983
Max McNab . . . . November 22, 1983 - September 10, 1987
Lou Lamoriello . . . . September 10, 1987 -

HEAD COACHES
Billy MacMillan . . . . 1982-83 through November 22, 1983
Tom McVie . . . . November 22, 1983 - May 31, 1984
Doug Carpenter . . . . May 31, 1984 - January 26, 1988
Jim Schoenfeld . . . . January 26, 1988 - November 6, 1989
John Cunniff . . . . November 6, 1989 - March 4, 1991
Tom McVie . . . . March 4, 1991 - June 5, 1992
Herb Brooks . . . . June 5, 1992 - May 31, 1993
Jacques Lemaire . . . . June 28, 1993 -

ASSISTANT COACHES
Marshall Johnston . . . . 1982-83 through November 22, 1983
Lou Vairo . . . . May 31, 1984 - May 6, 1986
Ron Smith . . . . August 6, 1986 - January 26, 1988
Bob Hoffmeyer . . . . September 17, 1986 - May 25, 1989
Bob Bellemore . . . . October 5, 1987 - August 20, 1990
Doug McKay . . . . February 4, 1988 - May 25, 1989
John Cunniff . . . . May 31, 1989 - November 6, 1989
Tim Burke . . . . November 7, 1989 - March 4, 1991
Warren Strelow . . . . August 20, 1990 - June 28, 1993
Robbie Ftorek . . . . July 9, 1991 - July 31, 1992
Doug Sulliman . . . . August 29, 1990 - June 28, 1993
Dave Farrish . . . . July 31, 1992 - June 28, 1993
Larry Robinson . . . . June 30, 1993 -
Jacques Caron . . . . August 9, 1993 -
Dennis Gendron . . . . September 1, 1994 -

DIRECTORS OF PLAYER PERSONNEL
Bert Marshall . . . . 1982-83 through November 22, 1983
Marshall Johnston . . . . November 22, 1983 - June 29, 1993

DIRECTOR OF SCOUTING
David Conte . . . . August 5, 1993 -

TEAM CAPTAINS
Don Lever . . . . 1982-83 through January 9, 1984
Mel Bridgman . . . . January 9, 1984 - March 9, 1987
Kirk Muller . . . . June 18, 1987 - September 20, 1991
Bruce Driver . . . . October 5, 1991 - September 24, 1992
Scott Stevens . . . . September 24, 1992 -

COACHING RECORDS

	SEASON	GAMES	W	L	T	PTS	PCT
Billy MacMillan	1982-83	80	17	49	14	48	.300
	1983-84	20	2	18	0	4	.100
	TOTAL	100	19	67	14	52	.260
Tom McVie	1983-84	60	15	38	7	37	.308
	1990-91	13	4	5	4	12	.462
	Playoffs	7	3	4	—	—	.429
	1991-92	80	38	31	11	87	.544
	Playoffs	7	3	4	—	—	.429
	TOTAL	153	57	74	22	136	.444
	PLAYOFFS	14	6	8	—	—	.429
Doug Carpenter	1984-85	80	22	48	10	54	.338
	1985-86	80	28	49	3	59	.369
	1986-87	80	29	45	6	64	.400
	1987-88	50	21	24	5	47	.470
	TOTAL	290	100	166	24	224	.386
Jim Schoenfeld	1987-88	30	17	12	1	35	.583
	Playoffs	20	11	9	—	—	.550
	1988-89	80	27	41	12	66	.413
	1989-90	14	6	6	2	14	.500
	TOTAL	124	50	59	15	115	.464
	PLAYOFFS	20	11	9	—	—	.550
John Cunniff	1989-90	66	31	28	7	69	.523
	Playoffs	6	2	4	—	—	.333
	1990-91	67	28	28	11	67	.500
	TOTAL	133	59	56	18	136	.511
	PLAYOFFS	6	2	4	—	—	.333
Herb Brooks	1992-93	84	40	37	7	87	.518
	Playoffs	5	1	4	—	—	.200
Jacques Lemaire	1993-94	84	47	25	12	106	.631
	Playoffs	20	11	9	—	—	.550

DEVILS' HONOR ROLL

TEAM/NHL AWARD WINNERS

Sharp Electronics Three Star Award
1982-83. . . . . Glenn Resch
1983-84. . . . . Mel Bridgman
1984-85. . . . . Doug Sulliman
1985-86. . . . . Greg Adams
1986-87. . . . . Alain Chevrier
1987-88. . . . . Pat Verbeek
1988-89. . . . . Sean Burke
1989-90. . . . . John MacLean
1990-91. . . . . Chris Terreri
1991-92 . . . . Stephane Richer
1992-93 . . . . Alexander Semak
1993-94 . . . . Martin Brodeur

Hugh Delano Unsung Hero Award
1982-83. . . . . Mike Kitchen
1983-84. . . . . Ron Low
1984-85. . . . . Dave Lewis
1985-86. . . . . Rich Preston
1986-87. . . . . Ken Daneyko
1987-88. . . . . Doug Brown
1988-89. . . . . Randy Velischek
1989-90. . . . . David Maley
1990-91. . . . . Bruce Driver
1991-92 . . . . Randy McKay
1992-93 . . . . Craig Billington
1993-94 . . . . Valeri Zelepukin

Fan Club Player of the Year Award
1982-83. . . . . Glenn Resch
1983-84. . . . . Mel Bridgman
1984-85. . . . . Kirk Muller
1985-86. . . . . Greg Adams
1986-87. . . . . Doug Sulliman
1987-88. . . . . Pat Verbeek
1988-89. . . . . John MacLean
1989-90. . . . . John MacLean
1990-91. . . . . John MacLean
1991-92 . . . . Claude Lemieux
1992-93 . . . . Alexander Semak
1993-94 . . . . Martin Brodeur

Fan Club Rookie of Year Award
1982-83. . . . . Jeff Larmer
1983-84. . . . . Pat Verbeek
1984-85. . . . . Kirk Muller
1985-86. . . . . Craig Wolanin
1986-87. . . . . Gord Mark
1987-88. . . . . Doug Brown
1988-89. . . . . Sean Burke
1989-90. . . . . Janne Ojanen
1990-91. . . . . Eric Weinrich
1991-92 . . . . Kevin Todd
1992-93 . . . . Scott Niedermayer
1993-94 . . . . Martin Brodeur

Ray DeGraw Memorial Good Guy Award
1982-83. . . . . Glenn Resch
1983-84. . . . . Dave Cameron
1984-85. . . . . Bob Lorimer
1985-86. . . . . Mel Bridgman
1986-87. . . . . Doug Sulliman
1987-88. . . . . Craig Wolanin
1988-89. . . . . Joe Cirella
1989-90. . . . . Ken Daneyko
1990-91. . . . . Brendan Shanahan
1991-92 . . . . Bruce Driver
1992-93 . . . . Craig Billington
1993-94 . . . . Bill Guerin

NHL Player of Month Award
10/87. . . . . Alain Chevrier

NHL Rookie of Month Award
3/88. . . . . Sean Burke
1/92 . . . . Valeri Zelepukin
1/94 . . . . Martin Brodeur
3/94 . . . . Martin Brodeur

NHL Player of Week Award
3/3-9/86 . . . . Kirk Muller
3/24-30/86 . . . . Sam St. Laurent
10/27-11/2/86 . . . . Aaron Broten
1/25-31/88 . . . . Bob Sauve